Salad Days

Salad Days

Exciting, easy-to-prepare gourmet salads

Zune and Heather Bampfylde

In association with

Tupperware

SACKVILLE
BOOKS

First published in 1987
by Sackville Books Ltd
Sackville House
78 Margaret Street London W1N 7HB

©Sackville Design Group Ltd

Designed and produced by Sackville Design Group Ltd
Typeset in Plantin by Sackville Design Group Ltd

Editorial consultant: Joan Jackson
Art director: Al Rockall
Illustrations: Phil Evans
Art editor: Joyce Chester
Home economists: Elaine Bastable and Lorna Rhodes
Photographs: Barry Bullough and Simon Smith

BRITISH LIBRARY CATALOGUING IN PUBLICATION DATA

Bampfylde, Zune
    Salad Days
    1. Salads
    I.   Title II. Bampfylde, Heather
    641.8'3   TX807

    ISBN 0-948615-00-1

Printed and bound in Italy by New Interlitho S.P.A. Milan

Contents

A salad is one of the healthiest and most versatile dishes that you can eat. Salads embrace an infinite range of cuisines and ingredients and are eaten all over the world – either raw, composées (cooked vegetables in a vinaigrette), warm à la nouvelle cuisine, dressed or undressed. Salads have no boundaries and know no seasons. With a flourishing international trade in salad vegetables and fruits, most salad ingredients are available all the year round and not just in the summer.

Introduction

Another advantage of salads is that they can be eaten as an appetizer, a main course or accompanying side dish or even as a dessert if they consist only of fruit. Thus it is possible to enjoy a healthy, nutritious salad in the course of every meal. For salads are a rich source of the nutrients we need in our diet. Fruit and vegetables contain many vitamins, minerals, trace elements and often complex carbohydrates and fibre as well. Adding fish, shellfish, meat, poultry, cheese, nuts, lentils, beans or a yoghurt dressing will boost the salad's protein content and provide a well-balanced meal.

Salads have been eaten since ancient times. In fact, the name is derived from the Latin word *sal* meaning salt. Probably the earliest dressings consisted only of salt, although olive oil, vinegar, lemon juice and wine were later mixed with the salt to flavour a salad. Back in the Middle Ages, salads were very colourful and elaborate affairs, built up in tiers of vegetables, herbs and meat and garnished with colourful edible flowers such as marigolds and nasturtiums or flowering herbs. In the nineteenth and early twentieth centuries, salads went into the doldrums in some Western countries although they continued to thrive in many traditional and ethnic societies in the Far East, the Levant, and around the shores of the Mediterranean and the Caribbean. Wilted lettuce leaves, watery tomatoes and dried-up cucumber did not help their cause, but now salads are in vogue again and chefs and cooks are experimenting with new ingredients, dressings and presentations to meet the growing demand for fresh and healthy food.

It is important that a salad should look visually enticing as well as tasting good. The quality of the ingredients used, the degree of freshness and the way in which they complement each other and are dressed and garnished all add to a salad's appeal. Presentation and the finishing touches – the final arrangement on the serving dish – are all-important. A beautiful salad is an edible work of art. For example, radishes and celery carved with a knife and left in iced water open up into roses, lilies and decorative tassels, whereas the skin of a tomato can make an attractive 'rose' garnish. Mixing different colours and textures also helps create a beautiful salad – the delicate tracery of pale green curly endive, the bitter dark-red radicchio with its white veins, the red-tinged fragile oakleaf lettuce, the crisp iceberg and fresh green Cos lettuces. Thus even in a leafy salad you can vary the degree of colour and crispness considerably.

Fruit in salads

It has become fashionable, especially in the United States to mix fruit into salads, thereby adding sweetness, interest and colour. Most fruit, whether it is the soft berry fruits of summer, the citrus and exotic fruits, peaches and nectarines, autumnal apples and pears or even cherries and plums can be mixed into a salad or their juices used in the dressing. Fruit and cheese make a harmonious combination within a salad, too. Try soft curd cheese with pear; Swiss cheese with grapes; cottage cheese with orange; mozzarella cheese with papaya or melon; and feta cheese with figs.

Winter salads

Salads make appetizing meals at any time of the year and need not be associated just with hot, balmy days in high summer. Winter salads are now becoming very popular, either served warm or tossed in a hot dressing, or using some unusual root vegetables and seasonal fruits that may seem alien to your perception of a traditional salad. Who would think of making a salad with celeriac, Jerusalem artichokes or red cabbage? However, served in a creamy, spiced dressing, they are the perfect accompaniment to the cold, leftover Christmas turkey or goose. A filling salad served with crusty wholemeal bread and a bowl of warming soup, or some cheese and tangerines makes a healthy meal even on the coldest winter day. Thus winter salads are featured (pages 102-113) with some original ideas for seasonal food. There are no problems finding fresh ingredients of the highest quality even in the middle of winter.

Serving salads

When should you serve a salad? As a first course before the main dish, as an accompaniment or as an after thought between the middle course and the dessert? Thoughts vary on this. In the United States it is customary to serve the salad after the appetizer, whereas in France and many European countries, the salad follows the main course to refresh the palate before dessert is eaten. In other countries, the salad is served on a side plate alongside the main meal. None of these are right nor wrong and basically whatever suits you is best. Now that more substantial salads are often served as the main part of a meal, the situation is even more confusing.

Salads make good snack meals, too. They are the healthiest 'fast food' that you can eat – easy and quick to prepare and nutritious to eat. Make them more wholesome by adding cooked beans or pasta, rice or lentils, sprouting seeds, cheese, fish, chicken or ham.

Vegetarian salads

Salads are beloved of vegetarians as there is endless scope for variety with vegetables, fruits, seeds, pulses, pasta, grains, sprouts and cheese. Throughout the book, vegetarians will find salads to suit their individual preferences and supply adequate nutrition. There is also a growing band of people who, while not totally vegetarian, choose to eat several meatless meals every week and there are filling, nourishing salads for them which contain good sources of vegetable protein.

In fact, vegetarian salads can be wonderfully versatile. Depending on their presentation and the ingredients used, they can be served as wholesome snacks, sensational appetizers, family meals or even as an elegant main course at a dinner party. More and more people are discovering that poultry, meat and fish are no longer the star turn of every meal – vegetables, fruit, grains and dairy products are all acceptable alternatives.

The right tools for the job

The kitchen tools and utensils you use in the preparation of salads can save you time and labour and help produce better results. There is no substitute for a set of sharp kitchen knives in a range of sizes. These are invaluable for chopping and slicing, paring, peeling and coring. Sharpen your knives regularly so that they will do the job fast and efficiently.

You will also need a sturdy chopping board to protect any work surfaces. Other useful tools include kitchen scissors for snipping herbs (far easier than chopping), a garlic crusher, a good potato peeler that you feel happy with, a sturdy grater, and a pestle and mortar for crushing spices and herbs and mixing ailloli in the traditional way.

A salad spinner is a particularly worthwhile investment as it speeds up the process of washing and drying salad leaves. You can purchase special sealed shakers for mixing dressings (otherwise use a screw-top jar). A set of measuring spoons and a measuring jug will help you measure volumes of oil and vinegar accurately.

Of course, you can also make use of electric kitchen aids and gadgets such as juicers, blenders and food processors where appropriate. Most processors come with special blades and attachments that enable you to chop, grate or slice vegetables in large quantities with the minimum of effort and fuss.

Salad vegetables

It is surprising how many vegetables can be used in salads, from artichokes to watercress. Many exotic and root vegetables are now eaten as well as the traditional lettuce and tomatoes. In fact, a good salad should be an aesthetically pleasing and delicious mix of leaves, herbs and interesting vegetables, preferably in a subtle but well-flavoured dressing.

Artichokes

The globe artichoke is really the flower head of a member of the thistle family. Related to the cardoon, it is indigenous to the Mediterranean countries. It looks attractive served whole with a simple vinaigrette dressing, mayonnaise or tartare sauce, or it can be stuffed.

Many people are baffled when they are presented with a whole artichoke and do not know where to start – they may even attempt to chew their way through the tougher parts of the leaves. However, only the bases of the leaf scales are sufficiently tender to eat. You should pull away the leaves, starting outside at the base of the artichoke and gradually working inwards. When you finally reach the centre, remove the hairy choke and then eat the *pièce de résistance* – the tender, succulent artichoke bottom. Artichoke bottoms for use in salads are also available in cans from most delicatessens.

Asparagus

The most prized vegetable of all, asparagus belongs to the lily family of plants. The green, white and purple varieties are all highly sought after and are an expensive luxury food even when in season (May and June in the northern hemisphere). Whereas the white shoots are popular in northern Europe, especially in France and Germany, the British, Americans and Italians favour the green and purple varieties.

Asparagus is usually eaten cold with a good vinaigrette or a lemon or orange flavoured mayonnaise, Sometimes finely chopped hard-boiled egg or strips of red pepper are used to decorate it and create a 'bundle' effect.

Aubergine

The handsome purple aubergine is known in the United States as an eggplant. Although some aubergines are

continued on page 12

Tomatoes
*Serve simply in a mustardy
vinaigrette with fresh herbs,
or slice into green salads for
a splash of colour*

Celery
*This adds crispness and 'bite'
to winter salads. It is the natural
partner to many cheeses*

Spinach
*Mix the raw tender young leaves
with mushrooms, chopped egg and
bacon in a vinaigrette*

Radishes
*The sharp, peppery flavour
and crisp texture make these
an ideal salad vegetable*

Lettuce
This varies in flavour and texture according to the variety used. It can be served with any combination of salad vegetables and fruits

Watercress
The hot peppery leaves go well with oranges, nuts, crisp bacon and cheese in a vinaigrette

Radicchio
The brilliant red-leaved radicchio is an Italian form of chicory. Slice a few leaves into winter salads

Fennel
The sweet aniseed flavour of Florentine bulb fennel complements tomatoes, Italian cheese and anchovies

Mushrooms
Raw button mushrooms are delicious added to salads or served in a soured cream or vinaigrette dressing

indeed round like eggs, many are elongated or bulbous. They have long been popular in the cooking of the Middle Eastern countries, and now they are on sale all the year round in the West, too. Although they are an interesting salad vegetable they are never eaten raw. They may be served stuffed and cold, or incorporated within a cold salad dish such as ratatouille.

One of the simplest aubergine salads of all is a simple purée of baked aubergine mixed with oil, garlic and lemon juice – sometimes referred to as 'poor man's caviare'. It is often served as a *meze* dish with pitta bread in Greek and Middle Eastern cookery.

Avocado

Popular in Mexican cookery, the avocado was cultivated for centuries by the Aztecs and, in fact, the name is derived from the Aztec word *ahuacatl*. Avocados come in a range of shapes and sizes, from the thin, smooth skinned green varieties, to the dark-green or purplish-black knobbly ones. There are even tiny elongated avocados which resemble baby courgettes. Although the intensity of flavour varies slightly, they all have pretty, pale green creamy flesh.

The avocado is one of the most nutritious vegetables you can eat. Although it is horribly high in fat (25 per cent), it also has the highest protein content of any fruit and is an excellent source of vitamins A, B and E.

Avocados add interest, colour and an exotic element to salads. Their natural partners are shellfish (lobster, crab, prawns), pineapple, grapefruit, nuts, salt beef and bacon. The ubiquitous avocado stuffed with prawns in a bright pink cocktail sauce is only one way of enjoying this delicious fruit – and not the best at that. Purists claim that it is best at its most simple and beguiling – halved, stoned and filled with vinaigrette. It is the essential ingredient in the Mexican dish *guacamole* and can be mashed into vinaigrette or natural yoghurt and used as a nutritious, pale green salad dressing.

Beans

Fresh and dried beans can both be eaten in salads. Tender young broad beans fresh from the garden can be served raw, whereas thin French beans are usually blanched or cooked until just tender before use. Most dried beans, including kidney, borlotti, soya, aduki, Lima and haricot beans, are also suitable. They just require soaking and cooking until tender. Mix the warm beans into the dressing of your choice while they are still warm to maximize their flavour. Beans are the main ingredient in many classic salads, notably *salade Niçoise* (French beans), *tonno con fagiole* (butter beans) and three bean salad (chick peas, kidney and French beans). They add colour, texture and fibre to a salad and are an excellent source of protein and B vitamins.

Beansprouts

Although these are available from supermarkets all the year round you can sprout them yourself at home. Crisp and crunchy, they bring a refreshing oriental element to a salad. They are also an excellent source of vitamin C. Mung beans, alfalfa seeds and whole lentils can all be sprouted quite easily.

Beetroot

Although beetroot has its devotees, it has acquired a bad reputation in recent years for 'bleeding' into salads and staining the other vegetables, especially when dressed with vinegar. The deep red beetroot is most popular in the Soviet Union and Eastern Europe, particularly Poland. It is also widely eaten in Scandinavia, usually mixed with soured cream or a sweet-sour dressing. Small tender beetroot has a pleasant nutty flavour and can even be grated raw into a salad. However, it is customary to cook beetroot in plenty of boiling salted water until tender. The skin is then removed while it is hot.

It goes well with apple, pickled herrings, onion, hard-boiled egg, spices and soured cream. It can even be dressed simply with a vinaigrette and fresh herbs to make an interesting side salad.

Broccoli

The tender bright green stalks of calabrese are better suited to salads than purple sprouting broccoli. They are usually cooked until just tender and then dressed with vinaigrette or served with a mayonnaise or hollandaise sauce. Chilling diminishes the flavour and spoils the texture, so they are best eaten slightly warm or at room temperature.

Brussels sprouts

You probably do not associate this member of the cabbage family with salads but when the sprouts are young and tender they can be eaten raw, especially in a creamy mustard dressing. It is important that the sprouts should be small and very green, not ageing, tough and yellowing. They taste good with grapefruit in winter salads.

Cabbage
This is a good standby for coleslaw at any time of the year. The winter white or Dutch are the most suitable varieties to use. However, even spring greens, Savoy and red cabbage can all be shredded raw into salads to provide a strong touch of colour and a crisp 'bite'. Cabbage goes well with apple, onion, bacon, carrot and nuts, in particular. Always rinse and dry well before use and shred finely. Remove the hard central core.

Carrots
These are usually grated into salads – either very finely with a vegetable grater or more coarsely with a potato peeler. They are particularly suited to winter salads where they add a splash of bright orange. An excellent source of vitamin A, grated carrot can be mixed into vinaigrette, yoghurt-based or soured cream dressings, with raisins, dates, nuts and fresh herbs, especially fennel, chives and tarragon.

Cauliflower
The creamy-white florets look very pretty in a salad or as crudités to be dipped into mayonnaise, aiolli, guacamole and other salad dips. Crunchy with a strong, distinctive flavour, cauliflower comes from the same species as cabbage and is packed with B vitamins, especially folic acid. It can be mixed into crunchy, robust apple and nut salads or served slightly warm in an oil and lemon dressing with oregano in the Greek style.

Celeriac
This bulbous winter root vegetable does not look very attractive with its thick, muddy, wrinkled outer skin and covering of hairy roots. However, be prepared for a surprise for inside there lurks a delicious, delicately celery-flavoured flesh which can be eaten raw, blanched or cooked – grated, diced or in julienne strips. Celeriac is often mixed with apple but the classic way to serve it is in Dijon mustard flavoured vinaigrette or mayonnaise.

Celery
Crisp and slightly bitter, celery is an excellent salad vegetable. It is the natural partner to cheese, an essential ingredient in a classic Waldorf salad, and adds 'bite' to turkey and chicken salads. Celery may be white or green, and generally the white winter celery harvested after the first frosts and covered with dirt is crisper and tastier.

Chicory
The white leafy shoots, or chicons, of this slightly bitter winter vegetable can form the basis of a winter salad. Chicory is known as endive in France and the United States. There is also a beautiful wine-red, tinged with white, Italian variety called *radicchio*, which is available from most good greengrocers and large supermarkets. The bitter chicons go well with ham, chicken, Swiss cheese, hazelnuts, walnuts, apple, orange, potato and smoked sausage dressed with a vinaigrette or a creamy dressing. Choose really white chicory. Although it looks attractive when the leaves are tinged with green, this is a sign of bitterness.

Chinese leaves
Another interesting winter vegetable with the texture of cabbage and a slightly celery-like flavour. It can be mixed into oriental style salads tossed in a sesame/soy dressing with peppers, lychees or pineapple. Choose firm crisp heads of Chinese leaf – reject any that are wilted or browning. You can slice off what you intend to use and replace the rest in the refrigerator in an airtight container or polythene bag. Wash and dry immediately before use and tear up the leaves by hand or snip with scissors.

Courgettes
These are commonly known as *zucchini* in Italy and the United States. The young fruit of the marrow plant, courgettes should be picked while they are small and tender. They may be bright green or, more rarely, yellow. The smaller they are, the more flavour they have although there is a tendency to blandness and they are usually mixed with tomato, onion, garlic or aubergine. They can be eaten raw, thinly sliced into summer salads, or stewed in Mediterranean vegetable dishes such as *ratatouille* which can be served cold. The simplest way to enjoy courgettes is to slice and blanch them, and toss in a well-flavoured vinaigrette with plenty of fresh herbs. The yellow flowers can be used as a colourful garnish.

Cucumber
You may see two varieties of cucumber on sale – the long, slender, smooth skinned hothouse sort and the knobbly,

continued on page 16

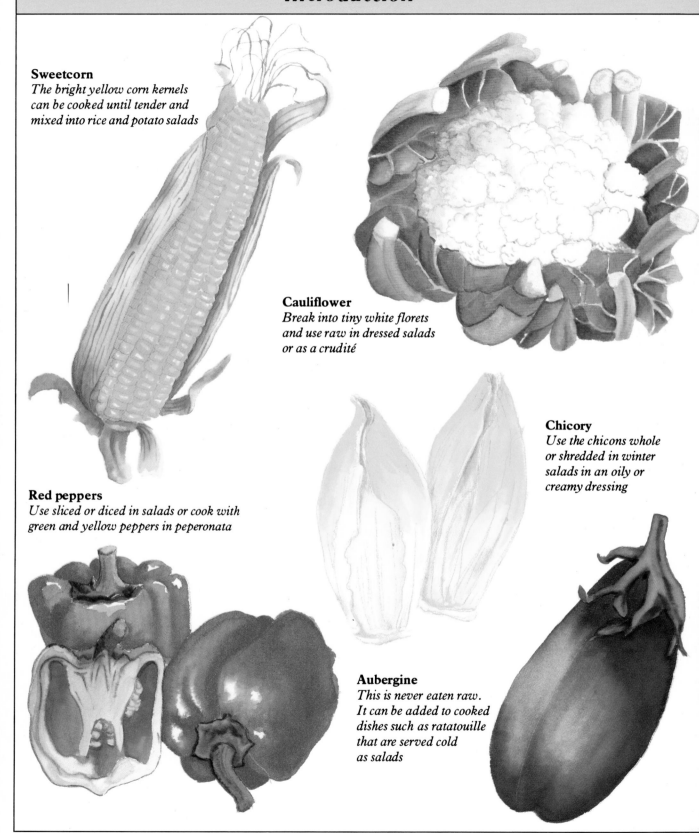

Sweetcorn
The bright yellow corn kernels can be cooked until tender and mixed into rice and potato salads

Cauliflower
Break into tiny white florets and use raw in dressed salads or as a crudité

Chicory
Use the chicons whole or shredded in winter salads in an oily or creamy dressing

Red peppers
Use sliced or diced in salads or cook with green and yellow peppers in peperonata

Aubergine
This is never eaten raw. It can be added to cooked dishes such as ratatouille that are served cold as salads

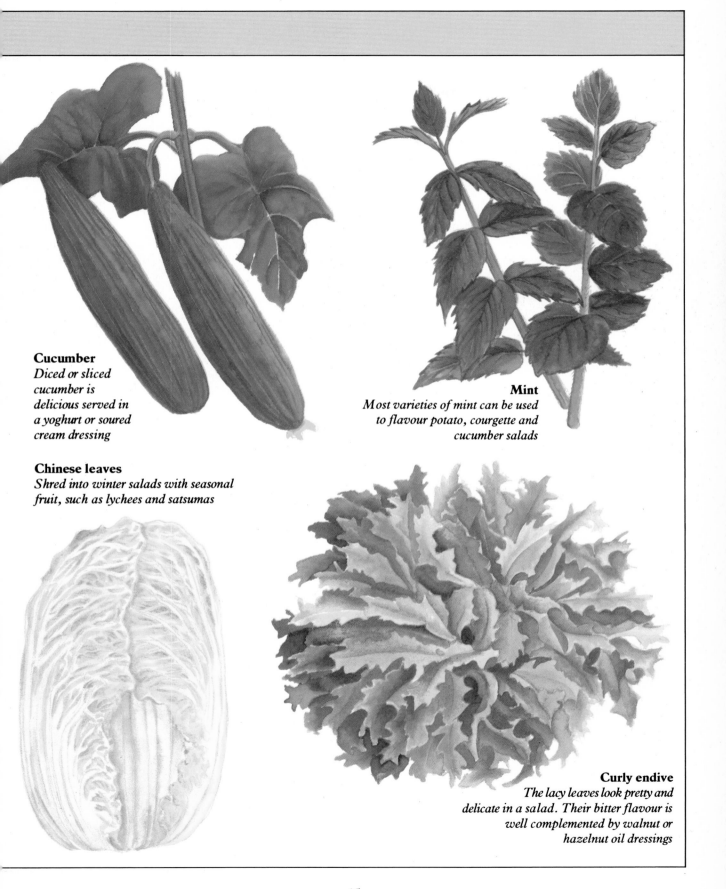

Cucumber
Diced or sliced cucumber is delicious served in a yoghurt or soured cream dressing

Mint
Most varieties of mint can be used to flavour potato, courgette and cucumber salads

Chinese leaves
Shred into winter salads with seasonal fruit, such as lychees and satsumas

Curly endive
The lacy leaves look pretty and delicate in a salad. Their bitter flavour is well complemented by walnut or hazelnut oil dressings

short ridge cucumber. Cooling and refreshing, sliced cucumber can make an interesting salad, either mixed with yoghurt, herbs and spices as in *tzatziki, cacik* or an Indian *raita,* or in a dill-flavoured vinaigrette. Avoid peeling unless really necessary as the dark green outer edge looks attractive. Remove the inner seeds only if large and hard. Always keep cucumbers in a refrigerator.

Endive, curly
Curly endive, or *frisée,* looks more attractive in salads. It has a slightly bitter flavour and complements radicchio, watercress and other salad leaves. It should be firm with bright green outer leaves and a fresh, crisp centre which is a paler shade of green.

Fennel
The sweet aniseed taste of Florentine bulb fennel is a delicious foil to milder salad vegetables. It should be really fresh and crisp, cooked *à la Grecque* or sliced or chopped raw into a salad. It complements tomatoes, anchovies and cheese, and is excellent served plain with just a vinaigrette dressing.

Leeks
Although they are usually eaten cooked, very young leeks can be shredded raw into salads. However, it is more customary to blanch or cook the leeks until just tender. It is important not to overcook them as they may become soft and slimy. Cooked, drained and dressed with a good vinaigrette, leeks are often referred to as 'poor man's asparagus'.

Lettuce
The most common salad ingredient of all can be delicious, crisp and colourful or a sad and sorry limp, tasteless leafy vegetable. It is generally best to avoid the floppy varieties and opt for crisper ones like Cos, Webbs and iceberg. The red oakleaved lettuce, although slightly limp, looks attractive and has an unusual bitter flavour. Freshness is all-important.

Corn salad (lamb's lettuce): seasonal in autumn and winter. The small dark green leaves are getting increasingly popular, especially in *nouvelle cuisine salads.*

Cos: also known as Romaine in the United States. This is a long, narrow lettuce with crisp, bright green leaves. It is much loved throughout the Mediterranean.

Iceberg: available throughout the year. This lettuce is very pale green fading to white and is particularly crisp. The hearts are delicious dressed with Roquefort dressing.

Webbs: another very crisp lettuce but larger and rounder than Cos. It is bright green with a firm heart and slightly crinkled leaves.

Mange-tout
These are also known as snow peas or sugar peas. They are really young, tender pea pods which are eaten whole in salads, either raw or blanched. They look most attractive in oriental salads in a sesame oil dressing. Unfortunately, they tend to be expensive but you only need a few pods to add colour, 'bite' and a special finish to a salad.

Mushrooms
The cultivated button mushrooms are most suited to salads, either eaten raw or stewed in oil with herbs and spices. Larger, open mushrooms are generally better for cooking. Look for tiny, tightly closed button mushrooms or with just a hint of the pinkish-white gills. Wash or wipe clean before use. Add whole, quartered or sliced thinly to a salad of chicory, apple, herbs and mayonnaise, or serve with watercress and orange. Mushrooms *à la Grecque* stewed in oil with coriander seeds and fresh herbs are particularly good. Or stew the mushrooms in butter and their own juices and mix with soured cream, chopped dill and lemon juice in the Russian style.

Onions
Spring onions, or scallions, are the sort most commonly used in salads. They are milder and more attractive than fully grown onions. They may be used whole, chopped, or sliced diagonally as in Chinese cookery. Many people just slice the white bulbs and discard the green tops but these can be trimmed and used also. Onions add sharpness to a salad as well as colour.

Palm hearts
These are usually purchased cooked and canned rather than fresh and raw. They are the edible terminal buds of a species of palm tree. Although they may not seem particularly appetizing, they are widely eaten throughout the Caribbean and the West coast of America and have an interesting mild flavour and good, firm texture. They are usually mixed into exotic salads and tossed in mayonnaise or a vinaigrette.

Parsnips

Another vegetable that does not sound like a typical ingredient for salads, but the sweet, nutty flavour of parsnips makes them surprisingly good in many winter dishes. Always use young tender parsnips if possible and avoid the older woody ones that may be frost-damaged. They can be grated raw into a vinaigrette with prawns and radicchio, or cut into julienne strips and cooked until tender. Toss in mayonnaise or soured cream with nuts and herbs.

Peppers

Red, yellow and green peppers add a spash of colour to any salad. The red and yellow are sweeter than the green but they are all rich in vitamin C. There are also red-hot chilli peppers which are much smaller and should be used with discretion. Served simply with a fine olive oil dressing and anchovies, skinned peppers are one of the most delicious salads imaginable with a bitter-sweet taste. Peppers also blend well with tomatoes, olives, aubergines and onions and are well represented in the salads and cooked dishes of the Mediterranean countries, especially France, Italy and Spain. A variation of the famous Italian *peperonata* is also a feature of Hungarian cooking, notably *lecso* which is served at room temperature as a salad.

Potatoes

Although they are never eaten raw, potatoes are great in salads – filling, nutritious and delicious. They were first brought back to Europe from South America by the Spanish conquistadors who discovered that they were the staple diet of the Incas. They are probably now the most popular and widely eaten vegetable in the Western world. They are particularly suited to robust, earthy salads and can be served either warm or chilled.

Whereas young new potatoes can be left in their skins, older ones need to be peeled. Choose firm waxy potatoes that will not crumble when diced. Desirée and Maris Piper are good choices. Potato salads are best dressed while still warm so that they really absorb the flavours of the dressing. Mayonnaise, soured cream, vinaigrette and yoghurt dressings are all suitable, especially when flavoured with fresh dill, parsley, chives or mint. Spring onions and crumbled crispy grilled bacon are good accompaniments as are pickled herring, salami, spicy sausages, anchovies and ham.

Radishes

These come in so many colours, shapes and sizes – dark red, crimson, pink and white; long and elongated or round and fat; tiny, medium or large. They have a sharp, peppery flavour that goes well with oranges and most salad leaves. Only the root is eaten – whole, sliced or carved into lilies and roses and left in iced water until they open up like flowers.

Spinach

This delicious green vegetable is probably a native of Persia and was brought to Europe by the Arabs. Serve raw in a vinaigrette or Roquefort dressing, or in a warm nut oil dressing ('wilted' spinach salad). Spinach goes well with most nuts, chopped hard-boiled egg, crisp bacon, mushrooms and shrimps.

Tomatoes

It is always well worth being selective about tomatoes as flavour, firmness, size and colour can vary enormously. There is no doubt that tomatoes are at their best eaten freshly picked when they are firm, slightly scented and well flavoured. If you grow your own tomatoes, avoid the common Moneymaker plants which can be found in garden centres everywhere, and plump instead for Marmande or another more flavoursome variety. Cherry tomatoes are also very sweet and look pretty in salads, or served simply with a Roquefort dressing.

Tomatoes partner most Mediterranean vegetables, especially onions, peppers, courgettes, olives and anchovies. The best and most simple partnership of all is tomatoes and fresh basil in a vinaigrette dressing.

Watercress

This shallow water plant has darkgreen peppery flavoured leaves and is delicious mixed with mushrooms, peppers, pears, oranges, Swiss cheese or walnuts in an autumn or winter salad. Roquefort, vinaigrette or yoghurt dressings are all suitable.

To enjoy a salad at its best, it should be really fresh and crisp. It is important to choose high-quality salad ingredients, especially fresh fruit and vegetables, that are bright, colourful and tender. Correct storage and preparation methods are also essential. Salad freshness can be sealed in in airtight plastic containers in the refrigerator until the moment comes for final preparations, dressing, garnishing and serving the salad.

Shopping for salads

Choose bright, crisp and firm salad leaves and vegetables that are free from wrinkles, blemishes and discoloured patches. Look for freshness – salad leaves should not be wilting at the time of purchase. They should be brightly coloured, young and tender – not limp and dull-looking. There is no definite correlation between the age and size of a salad vegetable. Thus a small tight lettuce may not be necessarily younger than a large, more open leafed one. Insist on handling the produce you buy – do not be afraid to test it for firmness or ripeness, to examine it for blemishes and look for bruising. This is one advantage of self-service supermarkets where you can browse freely. Greengrocers and market traders sometimes object to potential customers handling the vegetables on display.

Storage

Most salad vegetables will stay fresh if stored in the refrigerator, especially in the salad compartment at the bottom. Place in a plastic container or polythene bag to seal in freshness and flavour. There are some exceptions to this rule and special points regarding the storage and preparation of specific salad vegetables are listed below.

Preparation

You will be well rewarded if you take care when preparing salads – remember that salad leaves can bruise and discolour easily. All leaves and vegetables should be washed thoroughly in cold salted water to remove insects, slugs, dirt and traces of chemical insecticides. Pat vegetables dry with kitchen paper. After rinsing under running cold water, dry salad leaves in a salad spinner or shaker to remove every droplet of water. Wet salad leaves wilt quickly and any residual water can dilute the dressing in which the salad is tossed.

Never cut or slice a lettuce or any other leafy vegetable (spinach, curly endive, radicchio etc) with a knife. Always tear the leaves into manageable sizes with your hands to prevent bruising and discolouration. Discard any torn or bruised outer leaves.

Some fruit and vegetables such as avocado, apple, banana and celeriac discolour easily when cut. Brush the first three with lemon juice to retain their bright colour and prevent any browning. Immerse celeriac in acidulated water before using – just add a little lemon juice or vinegar to a bowl of water.

To skin or not to skin? More people are discovering that the skin does not have to be removed from many vegetables. For example, tiny new potatoes taste delicious in their skins, even when dressed with mayonnaise; and cucumbers and courgettes both look more attractive with the skin left on. Much of the nutritional goodness in many vegetables is located just below the skin, and peeling can diminish this. It is also worth noting that the skin is an excellent source of fibre, too. So unless a recipe calls for a vegetable to be skinned or peeled, leave it on.

It is the natural shape of a vegetable that usually determines the manner in which it is cut although there is a great deal of leeway. Peppers can be cut into strips, rounds or diced; tomatoes can be sliced or cut into wedges; carrots, celery, courgettes and other long vegetables look attractive cut in matchstick *julienne* strips.

Last-minute preparation

Just before assembling the salad, you can rub a cut clove of garlic around the bowl that is to be used to enhance the flavour and to achieve a subtle hint of garlic. Crushing a clove into the dressing itself is more obvious and stronger tasting for real garlic afficionados.

Always toss the salad in the dressing immediately before serving unless specified to the contrary. The leaves will wilt and lose their crispness if allowed to sit in the dressing for too long. Toss gently, turning the ingredients carefully to prevent them becoming bruised or breaking up. Every item should be glistening with oil or coated with dressing.

Artichokes: when shopping for artichokes, look for fresh green specimens and avoid any with darkening outer leaves. Cut away the thick stalk and place in acidulated water (water to which vinegar or lemon juice has been added to prevent discolouration) while you prepare the other artichokes. Boil in salted water until tender.

Asparagus: freshness is the most important quality to look for when buying asparagus. The tips should be intact and undamaged, and the stems fairly even in length and thickness. To prepare this superior vegetable, cut off the blemished, woody lower stalk and peel away the skin at the base with a potato peeler. Tie the stems in bundles and cook standing upright in boiling salted water for 15 minutes, or until just tender – not soft and mushy. If you cover the tips with a dome of aluminium foil, they will cook in the steam clear of the water. Drain the cooked asparagus and then dip quickly into iced water if using cold in a salad.

Aubergine: always buy bright shiny aubergines which are free from wrinkles and blemishes. To reduce their natural bitterness, slice into a colander and sprinkle liberally with salt. Leave for at least 30 minutes to exude their bitter juices and then rinse well under running cold water. Pat dry and use.

Avocados: never use one until you are satisfied that it is ripe as once cut it will not keep well. Put under-ripe avocados in a bowl with other fruit to speed up the ripening process. Test by pressing lightly with the fingers. Although it should be reasonably firm – not soft and squashy – it should yield slightly to the pressure.

Avocados discolour quickly once they are cut so all exposed flesh should be brushed with lemon juice before mixing into a salad.

Carrots: to prepare carrots, just cut off the tops and trim the bottoms. Scrape young tender carrots and peel older, harder ones.

Cauliflower: never buy cauliflowers that look overblown and discoloured. They should look, feel and smell really fresh. The florets should be firm and creamy white, the leaves bright green, and there should be no unpleasant odour. To prepare cauliflower, just cut out any blemishes (hopefully, there will not be any!) and remove the base stalk and outer green leaves. Carefully divide the florets and separate with a sharp knife.

Celeriac: when preparing celeriac, peel or cut away all the outer skin. Cut out any blemishes and slice, dice or grate. As it discolours very quickly indeed, it is important to pop it into acidulated water (water with lemon juice) right away. A good idea is to blanch it before use in this water to preserve its creamy colour.

Celery: store celery in an airtight plastic container in the refrigerator to keep it really fresh and crisp. Always wash carefully as it can be very muddy and strip away any stringy bits. Then slice across or cut into thin strips.

Fennel: to prepare fennel, cut away the base, outer sections and the leafy ends of the stalks. Wash and slice very thinly or dice. To keep it really crisp, immerse in iced water while preparing the other salad ingredients.

Leeks: choose young, slim leeks for salads – older, fatter ones are more suitable for soups and stews. They should have plenty of white stem. Trim the bases and the leafy green tops and wash thoroughly to remove any traces of dirt. Leave whole, slice in half or into sections before cooking until just tender in salted boiling water.

Lettuce: the best way to enjoy lettuce is to pick it fresh from the garden and eat as soon as possible. However, it keeps well in a sealed container in the salad compartment of the refrigerator, so look for a firm, crisp centre and green, not discoloured or wilting, outer leaves. When preparing lettuce, never cut it with a knife as it bruises easily. Wash well, spin dry and tear the leaves into manageable sections by hand.

Onions: if you use whole onions, you may find that Spanish ones are most appropriate as they tend to be milder. Red onions can be included most successfully in winter salads. If using whole onions, chop very finely indeed or slice incredibly thinly.

Peppers: all peppers should be cored and seeded before using. There are some recipes that call for skinned peppers – just hold on a fork in a gas flame until charred and blistered or place under a hot grill and turn occasionally.

Spinach: always choose young bright green leaves which look fresh and crisp. Discard any wilted dark ones. Wash well in several changes of water as spinach can be very muddy indeed. Dry and remove any thick stems.

Tomatoes: they are usually skinned before use in salads – either by dipping into boiling water or holding in a gas flame. Run under the cold tap and the skin will slip off.

Watercress: opt for bright green, healthy looking bunches which seem really fresh and immerse the stems in cold water up to the level of the leaves when you get home. Use quickly as watercress soon wilts and becomes discoloured and yellow. The vacuum packed sort keeps better and there is less wastage as it has usually been trimmed. Remove any long stringy bits and stalks before using and always rinse in cold water.

Salad dressings

A delicious dressing can elevate an ordinary salad into the realm of gourmet cuisine and it need not be difficult nor time-consuming to make. The quality of the dressing depends on the ingredients you use and it is always worth-while investing in fine oils, vinegars and mustards — for example, extra virgin olive oil, a good tarragon vinegar, fine aromatic French mustard, sea salt and freshly ground black or green peppercorns. However, the new breed of dressings uses other delicious and healthy ingredients in-cluding natural yoghurt, fresh herbs, soured cream, Roquefort cheese and oriental sesame oil.

Oils

Although the usual formula for a French or vinaigrette dressing is three parts oil to one part vinegar, it is generally agreed that this makes for a very acidic flavour, and that a ratio of five or six to one is more delicate and subtle. Avoid 'corn ' and 'vegetable' oils. They are very bland and highly processed, and will not do justice to a salad.

Olive oil: rich, robust and intensely flavoured, this fruity green or golden oil evokes all the scents, colours and flavours of a Mediterranean summer's day. It is the oil most commonly used in salad dressings but quality and flavour can vary considerably. Look especially for 'cold pressed' and 'extra virgin' oils.

Safflower and sunflower oils: these are blander than olive oil but higher in polyunsaturates. Although undistinguished and light, they are perfectly acceptable.

Sesame oil: beloved of the Chinese, this aromatic nutty oil is ideal for dressing oriental salads.

Walnut oil: the most highly prized oil of all. It often partners cider vinegar in dressings for warm and slightly bitter salads. It complements chicory and radicchio.

Other nut oils: almond, hazelnut and peanut (arachide) oils are being used increasingly by the new generation of young creative chefs. They tend to be delicate and subtle and must be refrigerated once opened.

Vinegars

Forget malt vinegar – it may be OK for fish and chips but not for uplifting a classy salad. Two or three good quality vinegars will last a long time, and the herb and fruit ones will look pretty on the kitchen shelf. Note that in Greece, the Levant and North Africa, lemon juice is often used instead of vinegar to impart a refreshing citrus tang.

Cider vinegar: this has a light apple flavour and is considered to have health giving benefits. Derived from apple juice, it is particularly popular in the United States.

Fruit vinegars: although pears, currants, gooseberries and plums are sometimes used, raspberry vinegar is most popular. It is particularly good for dressing warm *nouvelle cuisine* type salads. It is expensive to buy but you can make it yourself in the summer months by steeping a dozen or so raspberries in a good-quality wine vinegar.

Herb vinegar: basil, chives, garlic, mint, rosemary, sage, shallot, tarragon and thyme are all used to flavour vinegar and give it a distinctive, aromatic taste. You can make it yourself by infusing a white wine vinegar with a few sprigs of fresh herbs. Seal and use after a few days.

Wine vinegars: these are made from red and white wines. The best ones come from Orléans in France.

Salad dressings

Vinaigrette dressing

150ml/¼ pint olive oil
30ml/2 tablespoons wine or tarragon vinegar
salt and pepper
1 clove garlic, crushed (optional)
30ml/2 tablespoons chopped parsley, basil or tarragon
5ml/1 teaspoon Dijon mustard (optional)

Put all the ingredients in a sealed container and shake until well-blended. Makes 200ml/7floz.

Variation: Lemon vinaigrette
Substitute lemon juice for vinegar and omit the mustard

Oriental dressing

175ml/6floz sunflower or peanut oil
5ml/1 teaspoon sesame oil (optional)
30ml/2 tablespoons soya sauce
juice of ½ lemon
1 chilli, seeded and chopped (optional)
1 clove garlic, crushed
salt and pepper
1 spring onion, finely chopped
15ml/1 tablespoon clear honey (optional)

Put all the ingredients in a sealed container and shake until blended. Makes 250ml/8floz.

Greek Island dressing

100ml/4floz olive oil
juice of 1 lemon
15ml/1 tablespoon chopped chives
15ml/1 tablespoon chopped mint and oregano
1 clove garlic, crushed
salt and pepper
pinch sugar (optional)

Put all the ingredients in a sealed container and shake well. Makes 150ml/5floz.

Mayonnaise

2 egg yolks
5ml/1 teaspoon wine vinegar
5ml/1 teaspoon Dijon mustard (optional)
150ml/¼ pint olive oil
salt and pepper

Make sure that all the ingredients are at room temperature to prevent curdling. Warm the bowl and beaters, too. Beat the egg yolks, vinegar and mustard until thoroughly blended. Beat in the oil drop by drop and, as the mayonnaise starts to thicken, add the oil in a thin trickle and increase to a steady stream, beating continuously. Season the mayonnaise to taste. If, despite taking precautions, the mayonnaise still curdles, do not despair. Put a fresh egg yolk in a warmed clean bowl, and beat in the curdled mixture drop by drop plus some more olive oil. Makes 150ml/¼ pint.

Variation: Blender mayonnaise
Using the same ingredients, put the egg yolks in a warmed blender goblet with the vinegar and mustard. Blend thoroughly for 15 seconds. Pour in the oil drop by drop through the hole in the lid, increasing to a steady trickle as the mixture thickens.

Variation: Green mayonnaise
Mix 45ml/3 tablespoons chopped fresh herbs of your choice (parsley, marjoram, oregano, basil and tarragon, for example) and a small bunch of finely chopped watercress into 150ml/¼ pint mayonnaise.

Thousand Islands dressing

250ml/8floz mayonnaise
15ml/1 tablespoon chopped green olives
½ red pepper, seeded and chopped
15ml/1 tablespoon chilli sauce
2 spring onions, finely chopped
15ml/1 tablespoon chopped parsley
15ml/1 tablespoon lemon juice
salt and pepper

2 hard-boiled eggs, chopped
5ml/1 teaspoon sugar
2.5ml/½ teaspoon paprika

Combine all the ingredients until well blended and chill. Makes 300ml/½ pint.

Yoghurt salad dressing

150ml/¼ pint natural yoghurt
juice of ½ small lemon
salt and pepper
30ml/2 tablespoons chopped chives
1 clove garlic, crushed (optional)

Mix all the ingredients together and chill before using. This is more healthy and slimming than mayonnaise or most oil-based dressings. Makes 150ml/¼ pint.

Green yoghurt dressing

150ml/¼ pint natural yoghurt
salt and pepper
juice of ½ small lemon
30ml/2 tablespoons mayonnaise
60ml/4 tablespoons chopped fresh herbs eg. parsley, chives, tarragon, basil, mint

Mix all the ingredients together until well blended. Chill before serving. Makes 250ml/8floz.

Acidulated dressing

150ml/¼ pint soured cream
15ml/1 tablespoon lemon or lime juice
salt and pepper

Blend all the ingredients together. You can substitute ordinary double cream for soured cream, in which case use more citrus juice. Makes 150ml/¼ pint.

Avocado yoghurt dressing

1 large ripe avocado, stoned and peeled
juice of 1 lemon
150ml/¼ pint natural yoghurt
30ml/2 tablespoons mayonnaise
salt and pepper
1 clove garlic, crushed (optional)

Mash the avocado with the lemon juice and then beat in the remaining ingredients until thick and smooth. Serve quickly so that the dressing loses none of its fresh green colour. Makes 200ml/8floz.

Avocado dressing

1 large ripe avocado, stoned and peeled
juice of 1 lemon
50ml/2floz olive oil
1 clove garlic, crushed
salt and pepper
15ml/1 tablespoon herb vinegar
pinch sugar

Mash the avocado with the lemon juice to prevent any discolouration. Blend with the other ingredients until creamy and serve within 2 hours so that the dressing retains its colour. Makes 150ml/5floz.

Roquefort dressing

75g/3oz blue cheese eg. Roquefort or Danish blue
150ml/5floz soured cream or natural yoghurt
30ml/2 tablespoons chopped chives
salt and pepper
dash lemon juice

Combine the blue cheese and cream or yoghurt and blend thoroughly, thinning with additional cream or milk if necessary. Add the chives, seasoning and lemon juice and chill well. Makes 250ml/8floz.

A topping or garnish adds the finishing touch to a salad to make it look visually enticing and colourful. The sort you choose will depend on the salad ingredients used and the occasion. For instance, you might not bother to prepare pretty radish lilies or tomato roses to garnish a robust family salad but you might use them to decorate a special first course at a dinner party.

Vegetables, herbs, seeds, nuts, spices, croûtons and even edible flowers can all be used to lift a salad out of the ordinary class. They should always be added at the last minute immediately before serving and after the salad is dressed.

Herbs

These are probably the most commonly used of all salad garnishes, either chopped, snipped or in sprigs. They add a lovely fresh green finish and aroma to a salad. They are best used freshly picked to maximize their impact and this is possible if you grow your own. Of course, you do not need a custom-planted herb garden to enjoy fresh herbs. They are easy to grow in pots on a sunny window-sill, patio, balcony or roof garden. If you are really adventurous, you can have fun planting a herb knot garden and have the luxury of fresh herbs all the year round. Although you can use dried, the fresh sort have a more intense colour and look prettier. They can be bought in most big supermarkets when in season.

Basil: extremely pungent and aromatic, this herb favours a warm climate and is a familiar element in Mediterranean salads. Tomatoes are its natural partner, and the leaves are often left whole as they can look bruised and lose their fresh green colour when chopped.

Chives: their mild onion flavour and dark green colour make them a popular garnish. They are best snipped with scissors over the top of a salad. The pretty lilac flower heads can also be used for decoration.

Coriander: strong and pungent, it is often used in Greek and Far Eastern cooking. The whole sprigs, which resemble a flat-leaved parsley, look particularly attractive.

Dill: the feathery leaves add a delicate touch to egg, fish and cucumber salads. It is excellent in soured cream dressings and is commonly used in Russian, Eastern European and Scandinavian salad dishes.

Fennel: another feathery herb but although delicate in appearance, it has a particularly strong aniseed taste.

Marjoram (and oregano): this sweet, spicy herb is used in Italy, Greece and southern France, especially in tomato, pepper, aubergine and courgette salads.

Mint: most varieties of mint are suitable for use in salads, including applemint, lemon mint and pineapple mint as well as spearmint and peppermint. Mint can be used to decorate colourful fruit salads or to give a yoghurt-based dressing a lift. It is widely used in Middle Eastern dishes.

Parsley: the most commonly used herb of all. Ubiquitous if unadventurous, parsley has the advantages of a bright green colour, a distinctive flavour and being a good source of vitamin C.

Tarragon: its aromatic flavour complements fish and chicken salads. The French variety is better suited to salads than the Russian.

Thyme: this herb is better added finely chopped to a vinaigrette rather than to garnish a salad although it is widely used in Greek cookery.

Flowers

The notion of using edible flowers to decorate salads is an old one although unfamiliar to many modern palates. The large golden-orange courgette flowers are still a feature of Italian cookery, and flowers are now coming back into fashion, They can look incredibly pretty and colourful and some have an unusual flavour. Use them as fresh as possible and always add after tossing the salad in a dressing to prevent wilting.

Borage: the pretty bright blue flowers are often eaten candied but now they are used in salads, too.

Chives: the lilac flower heads may be left whole to decorate a salad or divided into florets and sprinkled over the top.

Courgettes: the golden-orange flowers are often stuffed with a rice mixture and fried in Italian cooking. However, they can also be used as an edible garnish for salads.

Marigolds: the distinctive orange and yellow flowers give sweetness and colour to a salad.

Nasturtiums: they add a vivid touch of colour ranging through yellow and gold to orange and crimson.

Nuts

Coarsely or finely chopped, flaked, toasted or whole nuts can be sprinkled over a salad prior to serving giving it a pleasant crunchy texture. They can, of course, be used in combination with a nut oil such as walnut or hazelnut. They are an essential ingredient in many classic salads including Waldorf salad (walnuts).

Almonds: these look most interesting when toasted to a golden brown and scattered over the top of a salad.

Brazils: chop roughly and use as a partner to oranges in salads. They are often found in vegetarian crunchy salads and winter recipes that call for a mixture of fruit and nuts when some fresh salad leaves are scarce.

Cashews: use *au naturel* – not ready-salted. They make an exciting addition to oriental salads and go well with chicken, apple and orange.

Hazelnuts: these taste good toasted in winter salads of chicory and celeriac. They complement apple in particular.

Peanuts: their strong, pronounced flavour makes them unsuitable in many delicately dressed salads. However, they are always popular with children and may encourage them to eat a salad they would otherwise reject. They also form the basis for a dressing used in the Indonesian *gado-gado* salad.

Pecans: popular in the United States, these nuts look most attractive in salads if left whole or halved rather than chopped. Again, they go well with fruit and slightly bitter salad leaves.

Pine nuts: these are often used in Italian, Greek and Middle Eastern salads. They look pretty and are an essential component of *pesto* sauce (sometimes the base of a dressing for pasta salads).

Pistachios: these attractive purplish-green nuts are a favourite in Mediterranean cooking and are now being used as a salad garnish. Most varieties are mild but some have a resinous flavour.

Walnuts: these taste best in salads when mixed with slightly bitter radicchio and chicory. They also complement fruit such as apple and pear. They are a favourite ingredient in spinach and bacon salads.

Seeds

Healthy and nutritious, seeds make an unusual but flavoursome salad topping or garnish. Like nuts, they can be browned before use to enhance their flavour. Just spread them out on a baking sheet and place in a warm oven to brown slightly. This will help give them a delicious nutty flavour. Pumpkin, sesame and sunflower are the seeds to use. They are all available from health food shops and are particularly good mixed into rice salads.

Croutons

These look attractive sprinkled on spinach salads and are always added to a classic Caesar salad. They can be eaten plain or flavoured with garlic and herbs. They make a tasty crunchy topping when mixed with chopped crisp-grilled or fried bacon.

Croûtons
3 thick slices bread, white or wholemeal
60ml/4 tablespoons olive oil

Remove the crusts from the bread and cut into cubes. Heat the oil in a pan and fry the croûtons until golden, turning occasionally to ensure an even colour. Remove and drain on kitchen paper. Although they are best eaten immediately, they can be stored for 2-3 days in an airtight container before they lose their crispness.

Garlic croûtons: add 2 cloves crushed garlic to the hot oil in the pan with the croûtons.

Herb croûtons
30ml/2 tablespoons chopped fresh parsley
15ml/1 tablespoon chopped fresh thyme
1 clove garlic
75g/3oz butter, softened
salt and pepper
3 thick slices bread, white or wholemeal

Place the herbs, garlic and butter in a blender and liquidize until smooth, or beat together until well blended. Season and heat in a pan. Remove the crusts and dice the bread. Sauté the cubes of bread in the hot herb mixture until crisp and golden. Drain.

Making garnishes
Always use a sharp knife when cutting vegetables and fruit. Choose good-quality ingredients that are not discoloured and free from blemishes.

Spring onion tassels
Trim the root end and some of the green end from the spring onion until it is about 7.5cm/3in long. Cut through each end several times, leaving a small area of white intact in the middle. Leave in iced water for an hour or so until the ends open up and curl attractively.

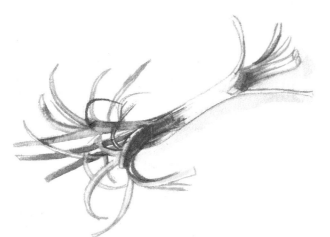

Tomato roses
Pare the skin off a firm red tomato in a 1cm/½in wide strip. Then begin curling the strip from the base, with the flesh side inside, until you have a tomato flower. Decorate with bay or basil leaves.

Radish lilies
Remove the stalk and cut through the radish 6 times downwards in a cross or star. Do not cut through the base itself. Leave in iced water until it opens like a flower.

Gherkin fans
Cut through a gherkin lengthwise several times with a sharp knife, leaving the base intact. Separate the slices gently to form a fan. Use as a garnish immediately before serving or the gherkins will become very dry.

Salads make an excellent first course – refreshing, light, piquant and not too substantial. Indeed, they whet your appetite for what is to follow instead of filling you up before you start a meal. You can serve a single appetizer or several small salads like the meze on pages 34 and 35. You can achieve a similar spread with an antipasto selection of Italian salads such as Italian prosciutto salad (page 32), tricolore avocado salad (page 37) and Sicilian mixed salad (page 48).

Salad appetizers can include meat as in Italian prosciutto salad (far left), fish as in Scandinavian herring salad (below left) and cheese as in Fruity cream cheese salad (below). The recipes are on page 32.

Scandinavian herring salad

3 rollmop herrings, sliced thinly
4 spring onions, chopped
2 red dessert apples, diced
75ml/3floz natural yoghurt
75ml/3floz soured cream
salt and pepper
juice of ½ lemon
30ml/2 tablespoons chopped dill

Mix the herring, onion and apple in a bowl. Blend the yoghurt, soured cream, seasoning and lemon juice, and toss the herring mixture lightly in this dressing. Sprinkle with plenty of chopped dill. Chill before serving.

Italian prosciutto salad

225g/8oz prosciutto (Parma ham), thinly sliced
1 large papaya, peeled, seeded and sliced
225g/8oz mozzarella cheese
few basil leaves
sprinkling black pepper
15ml/1 tablespoon olive oil

Wrap the prosciutto around the sliced papaya and garnish with sliced mozzarella and basil leaves. Season with plenty of freshly ground black pepper and dribble the oil over the mozzarella.

Fruity cream cheese salad

2 grapefruit, segmented
225g/8oz seedless grapes
45ml/3 tablespoons vinaigrette dressing
15ml/1 tablespoon chopped fresh mint
175g/6oz cream cheese
salt and black pepper
50g/2oz lightly toasted almonds
½ small avocado, peeled, stoned and diced
2 oranges, peeled and segmented
few sprigs watercress

Put the grapefruit and grapes in a dish and cover with the vinaigrette dressing with the mint added. Chill for 2

hours. Place the cream cheese in a dish and season well. Chop the almonds finely. Take rounded teaspoons of cream cheese and roll into firm balls. Lightly roll in the almonds and chill well before serving. Serve with the grapefruit and grapes, avocado and orange garnished with watercress.

Ratatouille

1 large aubergine
salt
1 large onion, chopped
1 red pepper, seeded and sliced
1 green pepper, seeded and sliced
2 cloves garlic, crushed
45ml/3 tablespoons olive oil
3 courgettes, sliced
450g/1lb tomatoes, skinned and chopped
30ml/2 tablespoons chopped fresh basil, marjoram or oregano
few coriander seeds, crushed
salt and pepper
pinch of sugar
1 small bunch parsley, chopped

Slice the aubergine and sprinkle with salt. Leave in a colander until it exudes excess moisture. Rinse well under cold running water and pat dry. Sauté the onion, peppers, and garlic in the oil until soft. Add the aubergine and courgettes and cook until golden. Add the tomatoes and herbs and simmer until the sauce is thick and the vegetables very soft. Add the coriander, seasoning and sugar. Cool and sprinkle with parsley.

Mexican stuffed tomatoes

4 large tomatoes
salt and pepper
1 avocado, peeled and stoned
½ green pepper, seeded and chopped
30ml/2 tablespoons chopped chives

1 clove garlic, crushed
1 chilli, seeded and chopped
15ml/1 tablespoon lime juice
15ml/1 tablespoon olive oil

Slice the tops off the tomatoes and scoop out the seeds. Season the insides with salt and pepper. Mash the avocado and mix in the pepper, chives, garlic and chilli. Blend with the lime juice and oil and season to taste. Fill the tomatoes with the avocado mixture and replace the lids.

Dressing:
60ml/4 tablespoons dry white wine
10ml/2 teaspoons soft brown sugar (optional)
10ml/2 teaspoons chopped parsley
15ml/1 tablespoon olive oil
salt and pepper

Prepare the avocados and brush with grapefruit juice to prevent any discolouration. Mix the dressing. Arrange the lettuce on 4 serving dishes and top with the avocado, and grapefruit and orange segments and the dressing. Sprinkle with parsley.

Mushroom and avocado salad

225g/8oz mushrooms, sliced
4 tomatoes, skinned and sliced
salt and pepper
2 avocados, peeled, stoned and sliced
15ml/1 tablespoon lemon juice
150ml/$\frac{1}{4}$ pint yoghurt salad dressing
$\frac{1}{2}$ onion, grated
30ml/2 tablespoons chopped chives
garlic croûtons to garnish

Place the mushrooms in the base of a serving dish, lay the tomatoes on top and season. Slice the avocados and brush with lemon juice. Make the dressing and blend with the onion. Arrange the avocado on top of the mushroom and tomato mixture. Sprinkle with chives and then pour over the dressing. Garnish with the garlic croûtons.

Avocado mousse salad

2 ripe avocados, peeled and stoned
300ml/$\frac{1}{2}$ pint whipped double cream
150ml/$\frac{1}{4}$ pint mayonnaise
7g/$\frac{1}{4}$oz gelatine
juice of $\frac{1}{2}$ lemon
pinch sugar
salt and pepper
few sprigs fresh dill
Tomato sauce:
450g/1lb tomatoes, skinned and seeded
50g/2oz onion, chopped
15ml/1 tablespoon olive oil
few fresh basil leaves
2.5ml/$\frac{1}{2}$ teaspoon sugar
juice of $\frac{1}{2}$ lemon
salt and pepper

Make the mousse: process or liquidize the avocado, cream and mayonnaise until smooth. Dissolve the gelatine in some warm water and stir in the lemon juice, sugar and seasoning. Cool a little and blend with the avocado mixture. Pour into individual oiled moulds and chill until set. Meanwhile, make the sauce: purée the tomato. Sauté the onion in the oil until soft. Add the basil, sugar, lemon juice and seasoning. Process or liquidize with the tomato purée and chill. Turn out the mousses onto pretty serving plates and pour the tomato sauce around each one. Decorate with sprigs of dill.

Avocado Jaffa

2 avocados, peeled, stoned and sliced
10ml/2 teaspoons grapefruit juice
1 lettuce, shredded
2 grapefruit, segmented
1 orange, segmented
30ml/2 tablespoons chopped parsley

Mixed leaf salad

1 small curly endive
1 radicchio
1 head chicory
50ml/2floz lemon vinaigrette dressing

Trim and wash the salad vegetables, separating the leaves. Spin dry and toss in the dressing and serve.

Taramasalata

6 slices stale white bread, crusts removed and soaked in water
2 cloves garlic, crushed
50g/2oz salted tarama (available in Greek delicatessens)
45ml/3 tablespoons lemon juice
75ml/3floz olive oil
1 small onion, chopped
black pepper

Put all the ingredients in a food processor and blend until thick and creamy. Serve with pitta bread.

Hummus

175g/6oz chick peas, soaked overnight
juice of 2 large lemons
2 cloves garlic, crushed
100ml/4floz tahina paste
salt and pepper
15ml/1 tablespoon sesame oil
pinch of cayenne pepper

Cook the chick peas until tender. Drain, cool and purée in a food processor or blender with the lemon juice, garlic, tahina, seasoning and oil. Serve, sprinkled with cayenne, with pitta bread.

Hummus

Taramasalata

Mixed leaf salad

Greek tomato salad

Cacik

1 large cucumber, peeled and diced
3 spring onions, chopped
15ml/1 tablespoon chopped fresh dill
30ml/2 tablespoons chopped fresh mint
300ml/½ pint natural Greek yoghurt
salt and pepper
squeeze lemon juice

Sprinkle the diced cucumber with salt and draw out any excess moisture. Leave for 15 minutes, rinse well and pat dry. Fold the cucumber, onions and herbs into the yoghurt. Season and add a dash of lemon juice. Serve chilled with pitta bread.

Greek tomato salad

4 tomatoes, sliced
few black olives
chopped fresh basil or oregano
50ml/2floz lemon vinaigrette dressing

Arrange the tomatoes and olives on a serving plate. Sprinkle with herbs and pour over the dressing.

In Greece, these mouthwatering dips and salads are eaten as meze – as a snack with aperitifs before a meal – or as a first course. Serve them with warm pitta bread (white or wholemeal), herb olives, pine nuts and chilli peppers for a delicious start to a summer dinner. Cacik, a minty cucumber and yoghurt dip, is often referred to as tzatziki.

Cacik

Coriander pepper salad

2 onions, thinly sliced
2 red peppers, seeded and sliced
1 green pepper, seeded and sliced
1 yellow pepper, seeded and sliced
45ml/3 tablespoons olive oil
1 clove garlic, crushed
5ml/1 teaspoon ground coriander
few crushed coriander seeds
1 bay leaf
4 tomatoes, skinned and chopped
150ml/¼ pint dry white wine
juice of 1 lemon
salt and pepper
30ml/2 tablespoons chopped parsley

Sauté the onion and peppers in the oil with the garlic. When soft, add the coriander, bay leaf, tomatoes, wine and lemon juice. Bring to the boil, cover the pan and simmer until the vegetables are soft and the sauce reduces (about 20 minutes). Season to taste. Chill and serve sprinkled with chopped parsley.

Artichauts à la Grecque

6 fresh artichoke hearts
juice of 2 lemons
100ml/4floz olive oil
675g/1½lb button onions
4 tomatoes, skinned and quartered
1 bay leaf
100ml/4floz dry white wine
few coriander seeds
salt and pepper
30ml/2 tablespoons chopped parsley

Trim and halve the artichoke hearts and brush them with lemon juice. Place them in a pan with the olive oil. Peel the onions and add to the pan with the tomatoes, bay leaf, wine and coriander seeds. Season and bring to the boil. Simmer gently for 20-30 minutes until tender. Remove the bay leaf and cool. Pour into a dish and chill well. Serve sprinkled with parsley.

Cacik and lettuce salad

1 small cucumber, grated coarsely
sea salt
300ml/½ pint natural yoghurt
2 cloves garlic, crushed
15ml/1 tablespoon chopped parsley
15ml/1 tablespoon chopped chives
30ml/2 tablespoons chopped mint
freshly ground black pepper
2 crisp lettuce hearts

Put the cucumber in a colander, sprinkle with salt and leave for 30 minutes to draw out moisture. Press gently to extract more liquid, then mix with the yoghurt, garlic, herbs and a good sprinkling of black pepper. Mix well. Chill for at least half an hour and serve on top of crisp lettuce. Garnish if wished with black olives.

Cretan tomato salad

3 large tomatoes, quartered and sliced
1 cos lettuce
2 small onions, thinly sliced
1 green pepper, seeded and sliced
½ cucumber, sliced
75ml/5 tablespoons olive oil
salt and pepper
30ml/2 tablespoons dried or chopped oregano
12 thin slices feta cheese
12 black olives, stoned

Mix the salad vegetables together in a bowl. Toss gently in the oil and season to taste. Top with the herbs, feta cheese and black olives.

Avocado Italian-style

2 large ripe avocados
100g/4oz ripe Gorgonzola cheese
100ml/4floz vinaigrette dressing
2 red peppers
20ml/4 teaspoons olive oil

Cut the avocados in half and remove the stones. Crumble the cheese into the dressing and blend together. Fill the avocado cavities with the Gorgonzola dressing. Char the skin of the red peppers under a hot grill or by holding on a fork over a gas flame. Skin them and cut in half. Remove the seeds and cut into neat slices. Arrange in a fan around each avocado and dress with oil.

Peperonata

1 large onion, sliced
2 cloves garlic, crushed
2 large green peppers, seeded and sliced
2 large red peppers, seeded and sliced
30ml/2 tablespoons olive or sunflower oil
675g/1½lb tomatoes, skinned and chopped
salt and pepper
pinch of sugar
few coriander seeds, crushed
30ml/2 tablespoons chopped parsley

Gently sauté the onion, garlic and pepper strips in the oil until tender (about 10 minutes) without browning. Add the tomatoes and simmer for about 20 minutes until the stew is thick and vividly coloured. Add the seasoning, sugar and coriander just before the end. Cool and sprinkle with parsley. For a hotter variation, add a chopped, seeded chilli or harissa paste to taste.

Tricolore salad

4 large tomatoes, skinned and sliced
12 slices Italian mozzarella cheese
4 spring onions, chopped
chopped fresh basil (or dried) and oregano
salt and pepper
1 large avocado, sliced
60ml/4 tablespoons olive oil
juice of 1 lemon
good dash herb vinegar
salt and pepper

Place the tomato slices on a plate. Arrange the mozzarella on top and sprinkle with the onion, herbs and seasoning. Overlap the avocado slices along the top. Mix the dressing and pour over the salad.

Italian cheese and pepper salad

2 yellow peppers
2 red peppers
225g/8oz diced fontina cheese
12 green olives, stoned
15ml/1 tablespoon chopped fresh basil
100ml/4floz vinaigrette dressing
freshly ground black pepper

Grill the peppers until the skins are charred, turning occasionally, and then skin. Remove the seeds and cut into thick strips. Arrange the peppers in a flower pattern fanning out from the centre of a serving dish. Pile the cheese and olives in the centre and sprinkle with basil. Dress with the vinaigrette and plenty of freshly ground black pepper.

Insalata di melanzane

2 large aubergines, diced
salt
75ml/3floz olive oil
1 clove garlic, chopped
350g/12oz tomatoes, skinned and chopped
10ml/2 teaspoons capers
8 black olives, stoned
pinch of sugar
salt and pepper
45ml/3 tablespoons chopped parsley

Sprinkle the aubergines with salt and leave for 1 hour to exude the bitter juices. Rinse under running cold water and pat dry. Sauté in the oil with the garlic until golden. Add the tomato, capers, olives and sugar. Simmer for 10-15 minutes until the sauce reduces. Season to taste. Cool and serve sprinkled with parsley.

Guacamole

2 ripe avocados, peeled and stoned
juice of ½ lemon
½ onion, chopped
1 clove garlic, crushed
¼ green pepper, chopped
2 tomatoes, skinned and chopped
5 coriander seeds
2 dried chillis, seeded and chopped
30ml/2 tablespoons plain yoghurt
salt and pepper and pinch of sugar

Mash the avocados with the other ingredients to a smooth, creamy purée or blend or process. Serve immediately with carrot, celery and red, yellow and green peppers cut into sticks, cauliflower florets, button mushrooms, spring onions, radishes and red cabbage.

Ailloli dip

6 cloves garlic, crushed
2 egg yolks
pinch salt and black pepper
300ml/½ pint olive oil
good squeeze lemon juice

Mix the garlic, egg yolks and seasoning with a wooden spoon. Gradually beat in the oil, adding it drop by drop until the mixture starts to thicken. Then add in a steady trickle, beating until thick and creamy. Add the lemon juice and serve as a dip with celery and cucumber sticks, sliced avocado and peppers.

Caesar salad

1 crisp cos lettuce
100ml/4floz olive oil
30ml/2 tablespoons wine vinegar
2 cloves garlic, crushed
60ml/4 tablespoons grated Parmesan
salt and pepper
squeeze lemon juice
few fried bread croûtons
175g/6oz diced ham or cooked bacon
2 raw egg yolks
6 anchovy fillets

Wash and spin the lettuce and place in a salad bowl. Blend the oil, vinegar, garlic, Parmesan, seasoning and lemon juice. Pour over the lettuce and toss with the croûtons and ham. Add the egg yolks and toss again until the salad glistens. Garnish with anchovies.

American wilted spinach salad

450g/1lb fresh spinach leaves, washed and trimmed
6 rashers back bacon, roughly chopped
75ml/3floz vinaigrette dressing
garlic croûtons to garnish

Arrange the spinach in a bowl. Fry the bacon in its own fat until crisp. Sprinkle the bacon over the spinach and strain the fat into the dressing. Pour the hot dressing over the salad and garnish with croûtons.

Wilted sorrel salad

6 rashers bacon, chopped
100g/4oz tiny button mushrooms, sliced
1 clove garlic, crushed
24 sorrel leaves, trimmed and washed
50ml/2floz vinaigrette dressing
1 hard-boiled egg, shelled and finely chopped

Cook the bacon in its own fat until crisp. Add the mush-

rooms and garlic and sauté quickly. Add the sorrel and toss in the bacon mixture. Toss the salad in the dressing while it is hot and serve immediately garnished with chopped egg.

Cold Hungarian lecso

1 onion, thinly sliced
15g/½oz lard
4 large green peppers, sliced
450g/1lb large, ripe tomatoes
15ml/1 tablespoon hot paprika
salt and pepper
5ml/1 teaspoon sugar
100g/4oz Hungarian spicy sausage, thinly sliced

Sauté the onion gently in the lard until soft. Add the pepper and cook over gentle heat for 10-15 minutes until soft. Add the tomatoes, paprika, seasoning and sugar. Cook for 20 minutes until thick and reduced. Stir in the sausage and leave to cool. Serve at room temperature.

Chicken liver salad

225g/8oz mange-tout
75ml/3floz sunflower or walnut oil
15ml/1 tablespoon tarragon vinegar
4 rashers streaky bacon, chopped
4 chicken livers, cleaned and diced
50g/2oz cashew nuts, toasted
4 spring onions, finely chopped
salt and pepper

Top and tail the mange-tout and remove the stringy bits. Blanch in boiling water for 2 minutes. Drain and toss while warm in the oil and vinegar dressing. Meanwhile, sauté the bacon in its own fat until crisp and mix with the mange-tout. Quickly toss the chicken livers in the bacon fat, adding butter if necessary. Do not over-cook them or they will be tough. They should be slightly pink and juicy inside. Mix into the mange-tout salad with the nuts and onion. Season to taste and serve immediately before the salad cools.

Warm chicken liver salad

4 rashers bacon, chopped
45ml/3 tablespoons olive oil
225g/8oz chicken livers, trimmed and sliced
45ml/3 tablespoons raspberry wine vinegar
1 head chicory, sliced
1 radicchio
100g/4oz corn salad (lamb's lettuce)
salt and pepper

Sauté the bacon in its own fat until crisp. Remove and keep warm. Pour the oil into the pan and add the chicken liver when hot. Cook quickly until tender – they should be pink and succulent inside. Remove and keep warm. Add the vinegar to the pan and stir over heat until well blended with the pan juices. Mix the salad leaves in a bowl with the bacon and liver and toss quickly in the hot dressing. Season to taste and serve warm.

Chinese sesame chicken salad

3 chicken breasts, skinned and boned
30ml/2 tablespoons soy sauce
4 sticks celery
45ml/3 tablespoons sesame oil
small piece root ginger, finely chopped
30ml/2 tablespoons toasted sesame seeds

Simmer the chicken in a pan of salted water with 15ml/1 tablespoon soy sauce. Remove when cooked and tender and slice. Slice the celery sticks diagonally and mix with the chicken. Blend the oil, ginger and remaining soy sauce to make a dressing, and toss the chicken and celery with the sesame seeds.

Tomato and avocado salad

15ml/1 tablespoon wine vinegar
45ml/3 tablespoons oil
salt and pepper
2.5ml/½ teaspoon sugar
2 avocados, peeled, stoned and sliced
juice of 1 lemon
4 tomatoes, peeled and thinly sliced
few fresh basil leaves

Mix the dressing: place the vinegar, oil, seasoning and sugar in a sealed container and shake well. Prepare the avocados and brush with lemon juice. Arrange overlapping as shown on a dish with tomato slices down the centre. Cover with dressing and garnish with basil.

Prawn stuffed avocados

2 avocados, halved and stoned
30ml/2 tablespoons lemon juice
225g/8oz peeled prawns
juice of 1 orange
1 clove garlic, crushed
100ml/4floz soured cream
salt and pepper
1 small jar lumpfish roe
4 sprigs fresh dill
12 whole prawns to garnish

Prepare the avocados and brush with lemon juice to prevent discolouration. Mix the prawns, orange juice, garlic and a little soured cream and season to taste. Fill the avocados with this mixture. Garnish each avocado with a spoonful of soured cream, a sprinkling of lumpfish roe, a sprig of dill and three prawns.

Pink grapefruit and avocados

2 pink grapefruit, segmented
3 oranges, segmented
1 ripe avocado, peeled and stoned
juice of $\frac{1}{2}$ lemon
30ml/2 tablespoons chopped onion
salt and pepper
pinch cayenne pepper
30ml/2 tablespoons natural yoghurt
1 bunch watercress, trimmed
30ml/2 tablespoons chopped chives

Place the grapefruit and orange in a bowl. Blend or process the avocado, lemon juice, onion, seasoning, cayenne and yoghurt until smooth. Toss the fruit in the dressing and arrange on a bed of watercress. Sprinkle with chives.

Cherry salad

1 iceberg lettuce, shredded
$\frac{1}{2}$ cucumber
30ml/2 tablespoons lemon juice
10ml/2 teaspoons chopped mint
450g/1lb dark red cherries, stoned
300ml/$\frac{1}{2}$ pint blue cheese dressing
50g/2oz pine nuts

Place the shredded lettuce in a serving dish and refrigerate. Peel and dice the cucumber and mix with the lemon juice and mint. Add the cherries and pile onto the lettuce. Cover with dressing and garnish with nuts.

Cheese and pistachio avocados

225g/8oz mellow blue cheese
30ml/2 tablespoons single cream
10ml/2 teaspoons chopped marjoram or oregano
pinch celery salt
black pepper
2 avocados, halved and stoned, brushed with lemon juice
1 bunch watercress
25g/1oz chopped pistachio nuts

Blend the cheese with the cream and herbs. Season to taste with celery salt and pepper. Chill for 1 hour. Prepare the avocados and fill with the cheese mixture. Arrange on a bed of watercress garnished with the chopped nuts.

Fig and cheese salad

1 cos lettuce
175g/6oz feta cheese
12 fresh figs, halved
few fresh dates or black olives
good pinch paprika
Dressing:
60ml/4 tablespoons orange juice
30ml/2 tablespoons oil
10ml/2 teaspoons wine vinegar
30ml/2 tablespoons parsley
salt and pepper

Wash the lettuce and discard the outer leaves. Arrange it fan-like around a serving dish. Put the cheese and figs in the well in the centre. Garnish with the dates or olives and pour the dressing over the top. Sprinkle the salad with a little paprika.

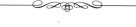

Beansprout fruit salad

225g/8oz fresh beansprouts
1 red pepper, seeded and sliced
4 spring onions, chopped
75g/3oz cashew nuts
225g/8oz chopped fresh pineapple
175g/6oz diced melon
1 avocado, stoned, peeled and sliced
15ml/1 tablespoon chopped parsley
100ml/4floz natural yoghurt
juice of 1 orange
good dash lemon juice
salt and pepper

Mix the salad vegetables, nuts and fruit together in a bowl with the parsley. Blend the yoghurt with the citrus juice and seasoning and toss the salad.

Watermelon and grape vinaigrette

550g/1¼lb watermelon
100g/4oz black grapes
½ small cucumber, cubed
45ml/3 tablespoons vinaigrette dressing made with
lemon juice instead of vinegar
30ml/2 tablespoons chopped mint
sprig mint to garnish

Remove the seeds and skin from the watermelon and cut the flesh into cubes. Halve and pip the grapes. Mix in a serving dish with the cucumber and toss lightly in the vinaigrette with the mint. Garnish with a sprig of mint.

Cottage cheese and orange salad

225g/8oz cottage cheese
1 avocado, peeled, stoned and diced
15ml/1 tablespoon lemon juice
45ml/3 tablespoons chopped chives
salt and pepper
4 large oranges
4 cooked prawns

Mix the cottage cheese, diced avocado, lemon juice, chives and seasoning together in a bowl. Remove the peel and all the white pith from the oranges with a sharp knife and slice thinly horizontally, carefully removing any pips. Arrange the overlapping orange slices on 4 small serving plates in a border. Pile the cottage cheese mixture into the centre and garnish each with a prawn.

Mango and avocado salad

1 large mango
2 avocados, peeled, halved and stoned
30ml/2 tablespoons lime juice
100g/4oz thinly sliced prosciutto
freshly ground black pepper
few sprigs watercess or lamb's lettuce

Cut the mango in half, peel and remove the flat stone.

Slice thinly. Slice the avocados and brush with lime juice. Spread the very thinly sliced prosciutto over 4 small serving plates. Arrange the mango and avocado slices alternately in the centre of each plate to form a star. Sprinkle with plenty of black pepper and garnish with watercress or lamb's lettuce.

Mycella pears

3 ripe William pears, peeled, halved and cored
15ml/1 tablespoon lemon juice
175g/6oz Mycella blue cheese
100ml/4floz natural yoghurt or soured cream
salt and pepper
pinch paprika
few sprigs watercress

Slice the pears thinly, brush with the lemon juice to prevent them discolouring and place on a serving dish. Blend the cheese with the yoghurt or cream, season with salt and pepper and pour over the pears. Sprinkle with paprika and garnish with watercress.

Autumn pear salad

4 large ripe dessert pears (eg. William or Comice)
juice of 1 lemon
2 bunches watercress
1 curly endive, shredded
45ml/3 tablespoons vinaigrette dressing
60ml/4 tablespoons mayonnaise
10ml/2 teaspoons lemon juice
paprika to garnish

Peel and cut the pears in half lengthwise. Remove the cores and brush with lemon juice. Wash the watercress, removing any woody stems. Prepare the endive and place in a large serving dish. Sprinkle with vinaigrette dressing. Lay the pears (inside down) in a circle in the centre. Mix the mayonnaise with the lemon juice and coat each pear. Sprinkle the paprika over the top. Garnish with the watercress round the edge of the dish.

Cucumber chartreuse

275g/10oz lime jelly tablets
hot water
300ml/½ pint cider vinegar
15ml/1 tablespoon caster sugar
few drops of green vegetable colouring
450g/1lb cucumber, peeled and diced
small cherry tomatoes to garnish
15ml/1 tablespoon chopped parsley

Separate the lime jelly tablets into cubes and place in a large measuring jug. Pour in hot water to the 900ml/1½ pint mark. Stir gently until the jelly cubes dissolve. Add the vinegar, sugar and food colouring and leave to cool to the consistency of unbeaten egg white.

Fold in the diced cucumber and when it is evenly suspended throughout the jelly, pour the mixture into a 1.8 litre/3 pint ring jelly mould and seal. Leave in a cool place until set. Turn the jelly out onto an attractive serving plate and fill the centre with sliced cherry tomatoes and chopped parsley.

Cranberry jelly mould

2 packets raspberry jelly
4 small jars cranberry sauce
dash wine vinegar
100g/4oz peeled prawns
30ml/2 tablespoons mayonnaise
15ml/1tablespoon natural yoghurt
squeeze lemon juice
few chicory leaves and watercress sprigs

Make up the raspberry jelly according to the packet instructions and, when cooling, mix in the cranberry sauce and vinegar. Pour into a 1.8 litre/3 pint jelly mould. Seal and leave in the fridge until set. To serve: turn out the mould and fill the centre with the prawns gently tossed in the mayonnaise, yoghurt and lemon juice with the chicory leaves. Garnish with watercress.

Asparagus vinaigrette

1kg/2lb asparagus
150ml/¼ pint vinaigrette dressing
2 hard-boiled eggs, shelled and chopped

Trim the asparagus and tie in a bundle with string. Lower into a pan of salted, boiling water and then cook gently until just tender. The asparagus should retain its fresh green colour. Drain and pat dry. Arrange the asparagus on 4 individual serving plates. Pour the vinaigrette dressing over the stems (not the tips) and decorate the stems with chopped egg.

Rice and almond salad

225g/8oz long-grain brown rice
6 spring onions, thinly sliced
1 cucumber, peeled and diced
150ml/¼ pint natural yoghurt
salt and pepper
juice of ½ lemon
75g/3oz chopped cashew nuts
15ml/1 tablespoon chopped parsley

Boil the rice in plenty of salted water until tender. Drain and rinse in hot water. Leave to cool and mix with the onion. Sprinkle the cucumber lightly with salt to drain off excess moisture. Leave for 10 minutes and pat lightly dry. Mix the yoghurt with the seasoning and lemon juice and pour over the cold rice. Stir in the cucumber and sprinkle with cashews and parsley.

Broad bean and rice salad

450g/1lb broad beans, fresh or frozen
50g/2oz long-grain brown rice
150ml/¼ pint natural yoghurt
1 clove garlic, crushed
pinch of paprika
25g/1oz pine nuts
salt and pepper
1 egg yolk
few well-washed spinach leaves
30ml/2 tablespoons chopped chives

Boil the beans until tender and drain. Do not add salt to the cooking water as this will harden the beans. Boil the rice in salted water until tender. Drain and mix with the beans. Mix the yoghurt, garlic, paprika, pine nuts and seasoning, and blend a little of this mixture with the egg yolk. Stir the cooked beans and rice into the remaining mixture and heat through very gently. Add the blended egg yolk and stir over low heat until the sauce thickens. Do not boil or the sauce will curdle. Cool and chill. Serve on a bed of spinach leaves sprinkled with chives.

Tonno con fagioli

450g/1lb cooked or canned butter beans
1 small onion, sliced in rings
200g/7oz canned tuna in brine, in chunks
30ml/2 tablespoons chopped parsley
Dressing:
60ml/4 tablespoons olive oil
15ml/1 tablespoon herb vinegar
juice of ½ small lemon
pinch sugar
salt and pepper

Mix the salad ingredients together in a bowl. Make the dressing and toss gently. Garnish with parsley.

Sicilian mixed salad

3 large tomatoes, skinned and quartered
175g/6oz cooked thin French beans
4 boiled new potatoes, sliced
½ cucumber, sliced
12 black olives, stoned and quartered
salt and pepper
225g/8oz tuna
45ml/3 tablespoons olive oil
dash wine vinegar

Mix the tomato, beans, potato, cucumber, olives and seasoning with the tuna. Mix the dressing and toss gently. Serve if wished with hard-boiled egg.

Egyptian ful medames

225g/8oz ful medames or fava beans
750ml/1¼ pints water
1 onion, chopped
2 cloves garlic, crushed
7.5ml/½ tablespoon ground cumin
100g/4oz red lentils
salt and pepper
30ml/2 tablespoons chopped parsley
30ml/2 tablespoons olive oil
juice of ½ lemon
2 hard-boiled eggs, shelled and chopped

Soak the beans overnight. Strain and place in a pan of fresh water with the onion, garlic and cumin. Bring to the boil and then simmer for 1½ hours. Add the lentils and cook gently for 1 hour. Drain and season. Garnish with chopped parsley and sprinkle with olive oil, lemon juice and chopped egg.

Bean and anchovy salad

175g/6oz dried haricot beans
1 clove garlic
salt and pepper
2 onions
30ml/2 tablespoons lemon juice
45ml/3 tablespoons oil
15ml/1 tablespoon double cream
5ml/1 teaspoon anchovy essence
15ml/1 tablespoon chopped parsley
5ml/1 teaspoon chopped mint
1 small can anchovies

Soak the beans overnight. Place in a pan with the soaking water and bring to the boil. Simmer for about 1½ hours or until just tender. Do not over-cook. Crush the garlic with a little salt. Slice the onions thinly and add to the beans while they are still warm. Stir in the lemon juice and oil. Blend the cream and anchovy essence, and add to the beans when cold. Mix with the herbs and adjust the seasoning if necessary. Drain the anchovies, cut in half lengthwise and arrange in an attractive lattice over the beans. Chill for 2 hours and serve.

Spiced lentil salad

225g/8oz continental lentils
1 onion, cut in thin rings
3 sticks celery, chopped
salt and pepper
2 hard-boiled eggs, quartered
1 lemon cut into wedges
8 black olives
Dressing:
60ml/4 tablespoons oil
60ml/4 tablespoons lemon juice
5ml/1 teaspoon Dijon mustard
1 clove garlic, crushed
30ml/2 tablespoons parsley, chopped
2.5ml/½ teaspoon ground cumin
2.5ml/½ teaspoon ground coriander
salt and pepper

Soak the lentils for 2 hours and place in a pan, adding more water if necessary. Simmer for 30 minutes, or until just tender – do not overcook. Drain and chill. Add the sliced onion and celery and season to taste. Mix the dressing and pour over the lentils. Chill for 2 hours. Garnish with the egg, lemon wedges and olives.

Fruity lentil salad

225g/8oz continental lentils
175g/6oz soaked dried apricots
2.5ml/½ teaspoon ground coriander
75g/3oz walnuts, roughly chopped
100g/4oz pineapple chunks
75ml/3floz vinaigrette dressing
30ml/2 tablespoons lemon juice
few sprigs watercress
3 fresh apricots, halved
2 slices pineapple, cut in chunks to garnish
8 stuffed olives, sliced

Soak the lentils for 2 hours. Cook for 20 minutes until tender. Add the apricots with the spice and simmer for 10 minutes. Drain and chill. Mix with the walnuts and pineapple. Add the dressing and lemon juice and mix well. Serve on a bed of watercress garnished with apricots, pineapple and olives, with cheese and pitta bread.

Fruity crab salad

350g/12oz cooked crabmeat or seafood bites
1 bunch spring onions, chopped
3 sticks celery, chopped
salt and pepper
150ml/¼ pint yoghurt salad dressing
juice ½ lime
1 head chicory
1 radicchio
2 grapefruit, segmented, or canned grapefruit
in natural juice
sprinkling paprika

Mix the crabmeat with the onion and celery and season to taste. Blend the yoghurt dressing and lime juice. Arrange the chicory and radicchio on 4 serving dishes with the grapefruit and crabmeat mixture on top. Dribble the dressing over the salad and sprinkle with paprika.

Fresh seafood salad

1 curly endive
100g/4oz corn salad (lamb's lettuce)
1 yellow pepper, seeded and sliced
60ml/4 tablespoons vinaigrette dressing
350g/12oz seafood bites or crabmeat
12 black olives
1 avocado, peeled and stoned
juice of $\frac{1}{2}$ lemon

Toss the curly endive, corn salad and sliced pepper in the dressing. Arrange on 4 dishes with the seafood bites and olives. Slice the avocado thinly, brush with lemon juice and arrange in a neat fan on each dish.

Artichoke and prawn salad

175g/6oz mushrooms, sliced
25g/1oz butter
15ml/1 tablespoon lemon juice
salt and pepper
225g/8oz prawns
75g/3oz walnuts, chopped
30ml/2 tablespoons chopped chives
45ml/3 tablespoons vinaigrette dressing
1 can artichoke bottoms
2 bunches watercress
15ml/1 tablespoon chopped parsley
4 lemon wedges

Sauté the mushrooms in the butter for 1 minute to soften. Add the lemon juice, salt and pepper. Cool. Add the prawns, walnuts and chopped chives. Mix with the dressing. Drain the artichokes and fill with the mixture. Chill for 2 hours and serve on a bed of watercress. Sprinkle with the chopped parsley and garnish with the lemon wedges.

Mediterranean squid salad

450g/1lb squid
45ml/3 tablespoons oil
3 tomatoes, skinned, seeded and chopped
1 green pepper, seeded and chopped
4 spring onions, chopped
75ml/3floz vinaigrette dressing
juice of $\frac{1}{2}$ lemon
8 black olives
30ml/2 tablespoons chopped parsley

Clean the squid by separating the hood and tentacles. Discard the intestines, brain and spine. Peel off the purplish outer skin. Rinse well inside and out under running cold water and pat dry. Cut the hood into thin rings and the tentacles into chunks. Cook quickly in the oil over very high heat until just tender. Cool and mix with the tomato, pepper and onion. Toss in the dressing and lemon juice. Chill well and serve garnished with olives and parsley.

Italian seafood salad

225g/8oz cooked prawns
1 squid, cleaned, cooked and sliced
20 cooked mussels (or canned)
16 cooked clams (or canned)
8 black olives, stoned and quartered
1 small red pepper
60ml/4 tablespoons olive oil
15ml/1 tablespoon lemon juice
2 cloves garlic, crushed
salt and pepper
chopped fresh oregano or marjoram

Put the seafood and olives in a bowl. Grill the pepper until charred and skin it. Cut into strips and add to the other salad ingredients. Mix the oil, lemon juice, garlic, seasoning and herbs to make the dressing and toss well. Chill before eating.

Scallop mayonnaise

8 scallops
1 head curly endive, shredded
salt and pepper
15ml/1 tablespoon lemon juice
300ml/½ pint green mayonnaise
15ml/1 tablespoon chopped fresh dill

Steam the scallops and cool. Cut the white parts and corals into large slices. Arrange the shredded endive on a serving dish. Add the seasoning and lemon juice to the mayonnaise and lightly toss the endive. Lay the scallops on top, season lightly and sprinkle with lemon juice and chopped fresh dill.

Avocado and tuna salad

1 can tuna, drained and diced
1 small onion, grated
1 green pepper, diced
2 avocados, halved and stoned
15ml/1 tablespoon lemon juice
1 lettuce, shredded
60ml/4 tablespoons vinaigrette dressing
6 sliced black olives

Prepare the tuna and mix with the onion and green pepper. Just before serving, prepare the avocados and brush with lemon juice. Arrange the shredded lettuce on 4 serving plates with an avocado on each. Fill with the tuna mixture to overflowing. Pour over the dressing and garnish with the olives.

Melon salad

1 large canteloupe melon
3 spring onions, sliced
1 carrot, grated
½ Webbs lettuce or curly endive, shredded
1 orange, segmented
225g/8oz peeled prawns
90ml/6 tablespoons vinaigrette dressing
2 hard-boiled eggs, quartered
6 radish flowers
12 black olives

Cut the melon in half, take out the seeds and, using a food baller, remove the flesh. Reserve any juice to add to the dressing, and keep the melon shells. Place the onion, carrot and shredded lettuce or curly endive in a dish. Add the orange and two-thirds of the prawns, keeping the remainder for the garnish. Add the dressing and the melon balls. Mix well and refrigerate for 2 hours to chill slightly. Fill the hollow melon shells with the mixture. Garnish with the eggs, radishes, olives and prawns.

Mediterranean tomato and tuna salad

4 large tomatoes, sliced thinly
4 hard-boiled eggs, sliced
225g/8oz tuna, cut in chunks
60ml/4 tablespoons olive oil
15ml/1 tablespoon herb vinegar
salt and pepper
30ml/2 tablespoons chopped chives

Arrange the tomato and egg slices in an overlapping circle. Fill the hole in the centre with tuna and make a dressing with the oil, vinegar and seasoning. Scatter with plenty of chopped fresh chives.

Main courses

More substantial salads can be served as a main course, especially on a hot summer's day when you feel like a light meal. Meat, fish and shellfish can be added to make a salad more filling. Vegetarians can mix such delicious foods as beans, grains, rice, pasta, cheese and eggs into fresh vegetables and fruit to boost the protein content. The range of main course salads is endless and you can have fun experimenting with your favourite ingredients. Make use of whatever is seasonal and plentiful.

Salad brochettes (far left) and fish escabeche (below left) are unusual main course salads whereas Salade Nicoise (below) is among the classic Mediterranean cold dishes. The recipes are on pages 56 and 57.

Salad brochettes

4 small cherry tomatoes
8 chunks green pepper
8 chunks red pepper
8 chunks cucumber
12 chunks pineapple
350g/12oz cooked chicken, cut in chunks
250ml/8floz natural yoghurt
45ml/3 tablespoons mayonnaise
squeeze lemon juice
2.5ml/½ teaspoon Chinese curry powder
30ml/2 tablespoons chopped parsley

Thread all the salad and fruit ingredients and the chicken onto 8 kebab skewers. Mix the remaining ingredients to make a spicy mayonnaise and serve the brochettes sprinkled with parsley.

Marinated kipper salad

4 kipper fillets, skinned
15ml/1 tablespoon lemon juice
60ml/4 tablespoons olive oil
1 red skinned onion, thinly sliced
1 bay leaf
1 crisp iceberg lettuce, shredded
2 red dessert apples, cored and diced
2 celery sticks, sliced
¼ cucumber, diced
8 small cooked new potatoes, cubed
salt and black pepper
15ml/1 tablespoon snipped chives

Cut the kipper fillets into thin strips and put into a shallow container with the lemon juice, oil, onion and bay leaf. Cover and marinate for 24 hours. Arrange the lettuce on a serving dish. Mix the apple, celery, cucumber, potato and kippers in the marinade, discarding the bay leaf. Season and arrange on top of the lettuce. Sprinkle with chopped chives before serving.

Fish escabeche

8 fillets of sole, flounder or any white fish
salt and pepper
60ml/4 tablespoons olive oil
1 bay leaf
juice of 3 lemons or limes
juice of 2 oranges
1 orange, peeled and thinly sliced
15ml/1 tablespoon chopped green pepper
3 spring onions, chopped
pinch of ground nutmeg
50g/2oz peeled prawns
1 avocado, peeled, stoned and thinly sliced (optional)

Season the skinned and boned fish fillets and cut into thin strips. Fry them in half the olive oil until just cooked and golden-brown. Drain and place in a shallow dish with the bay leaf. Pour the fruit juice and remaining olive oil over the top. Arrange the orange and green pepper over the fish and sprinkle with spring onion, seasoning and nutmeg. Cover the dish and chill for at least 12 hours. Add a little more olive oil and remove the bay leaf just before serving. Garnish with shrimps and sliced avocado (optional).

Scandinavian dill kippers

8 kipper fillets, cut in strips
2 large boiled potatoes, cubed
2 red dessert apples, cored and diced
3 spring onions, chopped
100g/4oz cooked beetroot, diced
100ml/4floz soured cream
15ml/1 tablespoon mayonnaise
juice of ½ small lemon
salt and sugar
few sprigs fresh dill

Mix the kipper with the potato, apple, onion and beetroot. Blend the soured cream and mayonnaise with the lemon juice and season to taste. Chop some sprigs of dill (retaining 2 or 3 for the garnish) and add to the dressing. Toss the salad in the dressing and garnish with the remaining sprigs of dill.

Riviera fish salad

225g/8oz crabmeat
225g/8oz shelled cooked prawns
225g/8oz cooked mussels
1 green pepper, seeded and diced
3 spring onions, chopped
100ml/4floz mayonnaise
juice of $\frac{1}{2}$ lemon
2.5ml/$\frac{1}{2}$ teaspoon powdered saffron
salt and pepper
1 curly endive heart or 3 heads corn salad
15ml/1 tablespoon chopped chives

Mix the crabmeat, prawns, mussels, pepper and onion in a bowl. Blend the mayonnaise, lemon juice and saffron to a pale yellow creamy dressing. Season to taste. Toss the salad lightly in this dressing. Pile the salad onto some endive or corn salad and sprinkle with chives.

Salade Nicoise

225g/8oz thin French beans
2 medium-sized waxy potatoes
3 spring onions, chopped
225g/8oz tomatoes, quartered
100g/4oz garlic sausage, cut in chunks
200g/7oz canned tuna fish, drained and cut in chunks
3 hard-boiled eggs, shelled and finely chopped
12 black olives
45ml/3 tablespoons chopped parsley
Dressing:
60ml/4 tablespoons olive oil
15ml/1 tablespoon wine vinegar
juice of $\frac{1}{2}$ lemon
1.25ml/$\frac{1}{4}$ teaspoon Dijon mustard
salt and pepper

Top and tail the French beans and cook in boiling salted water until *just* tender with the pan uncovered to retain the fresh, green colour. Drain and cool. Peel the potatoes and cook in boiling water until tender. Use tiny new potatoes if preferred. Cool and cut into chunks. Mix the beans and potatoes with the onion, tomato, garlic sausage and tuna. Mix the dressing and toss the salad. Arrange on a serving platter within a border of chopped egg. Garnish with the olives and parsley.

Sardine salad

2 cans sardines in oil
1 cucumber, diced, salted and drained
60ml/4 tablespoons vinaigrette dressing
15ml/1 tablespoon lemon juice
1 onion, cut into thin rings
5ml/1 teaspoon turmeric
225g/8oz cooked long-grain rice
salt and pepper
1 can anchovy fillets
chopped parsley
few radish roses

Drain the sardines. Rinse the prepared cucumber and pat dry with kitchen paper. Mix the dressing and lemon juice and pour over the onion and cucumber. Fork the turmeric into the cooked rice and season to taste. Place the rice on a serving dish with the onion and cucumber. Arrange the sardines on top and garnish with anchovies, chopped parsley and radish roses.

Scampi salad

450g/1lb shelled scampi
50g/2oz butter
225g/8oz pasta shells
black pepper
1 small green pepper, seeded and diced
300ml/½ pint lemon mayonnaise
1 cos lettuce
4 hard-boiled eggs, quartered
few watercress sprigs
sprinkling paprika
8 whole cooked scampi to garnish

Sauté the scampi in the butter for 2-3 minutes. Season with pepper and drain on kitchen paper. Cook the pasta until tender and drain. Cool and mix with the scampi, green pepper and lemon mayonnaise (commercial sort or mix 30ml/2 tablespoons lemon juice into the same volume of mayonnaise). Arrange the cos lettuce on 4 serving plates with the scampi mixture on top. Garnish with egg and watercress. Sprinkle with paprika and garnish with scampi.

Main courses

Cucumber and mackerel salad

2 bunches radishes
1 large cucumber
45ml/3 tablespoons oil
30ml/2 tablespoons lemon juice
10ml/2 teaspoons wine vinegar
salt and pepper
1 crisp lettuce, shredded
4 fillets smoked mackerel
1 lemon, sliced
15ml/1 tablespoon chopped chives

Slice the radishes and set aside. Peel and dice the cucumber (not too small), sprinkle with salt and leave for 15 minutes. Drain, wash and pat dry with kitchen paper. Mix with the radish. Make the dressing: place the oil, lemon juice, vinegar and seasoning in a sealed container and shake well. Pour over the radish and cucumber. Just before serving, arrange the lettuce on a serving dish, top with the cucumber and radish mixture and arrange the mackerel fillets on top. Garnish with lemon slices and chopped chives.

Greek plaki salad

4 white fish steaks
juice of $\frac{1}{2}$ lemon
1 onion, chopped
1 small bulb fennel, chopped
2 cloves garlic, crushed
45ml/3 tablespoons olive oil
450g/1lb tomatoes, skinned and chopped
pinch of sugar
5ml/1 teaspoon dried oregano
sprigs fresh thyme and rosemary
150ml/5floz red wine
50g/2oz black olives
salt and pepper
30ml/2 tablespoons chopped parsley

Sprinkle the fish steaks with lemon juice in an ovenproof dish. Sauté the onion, fennel and garlic in the oil until soft. Add the tomato, sugar, herbs and red wine and cook gently for a few minutes. Pour over the fish, add the olives and season. Bake in a preheated oven at 180°C, 350°F, gas 4 for 30 minutes. Cool and sprinkle with parsley. Serve at room temperature with green salad.

Mixed seafood salad

1 small can salmon, drained
175g/6oz prawns or shrimps, shelled
100g/4oz crabmeat
small jar cockles or mussels
2 bunches watercress
15ml/1 tablespoon chopped chives
1 large orange, peeled and sliced
12 black olives
150ml/$\frac{1}{4}$ pint green mayonnaise
60ml/4 tablespoons natural yoghurt
juice $\frac{1}{2}$ lemon

Mix the seafood with the watercress, herbs, orange slices and black olives. Toss gently in the green mayonnaise blended with the yoghurt and lemon juice.

Salmon mayonnaise

4 salmon steaks
2.5ml/$\frac{1}{2}$ teaspoon dill
salt and pepper
150ml/$\frac{1}{4}$ pint white wine
25g/1oz butter
2 shallots or $\frac{1}{2}$ onion, grated
1 cucumber, peeled, seeded and finely diced
100g/4oz peeled prawns
300ml/$\frac{1}{2}$ pint thick mayonnaise
1 bunch watercress
lemon wedges
10ml/2 teaspoons chopped parsley

Place the salmon in an ovenproof dish and sprinkle with the dill and seasoning. Pour in the wine and dot with butter. Cover with foil and cook at 180°C, 350°F, gas 4 for about 15 minutes or until tender. Drain and reserve the fish liquor. Remove the centre bone and place the steaks on a serving dish. Put the shallots and cucumber in a pan, pour the fish liquor over, season lightly and bring to the boil. Simmer for 2 minutes, drain and put to one side. Fill the centre of each salmon steak with the mixture and press together. Use a wooden cocktail stick if necessary to secure. Cover and leave to cool. When the reserved liquor is cold, mix with the prawns and chill. To serve, carefully coat the salmon with the mayonnaise. Garnish with the drained prawns and watercress. Serve with the lemon dipped in parsley.

Danish gammon salad

225g/8oz red cabbage, finely shredded
30ml/2 tablespoons wine vinegar
1 large onion, preferably Spanish, finely sliced
30ml/2 tablespoons oil
3 rashers Danish gammon, cut in thin strips
100g/4oz mushrooms, wiped and sliced
black pepper
45ml/3 tablespoons vinaigrette dressing
garlic croûtons
10ml/2 teaspoons chopped parsley

Place the prepared cabbage in a dish. Heat the vinegar to boiling, pour over the cabbage and stir well. This will change the colour of the cabbage, turning it bright red. Leave to cool. Add the sliced onion to the cabbage. Heat the oil in a pan and sauté the gammon. Remove and cool. Add the mushrooms to the pan, just toss in the oil for ½ minute, add the pepper and mix with the gammon. Leave to cool. Pour the dressing over the cabbage and fold in the gammon mixture. Garnish with garlic croûtons and chopped parsley.

Ham and pineapple salad

1 fresh pineapple, halved
225g/8oz cherries, stoned
225g/8oz cooked Danish gammon, diced
25g/1oz walnuts, roughly chopped
1 bunch watercress

Dressing:
30ml/2 tablespoons orange juice
30ml/2 tablespoons white wine
5ml/1 teaspoon lemon juice
5ml/1 teaspoon soft brown sugar
5ml/1 teaspoon chopped mint
5ml/1 teaspoon chopped chives
salt and pepper

Prepare the pineapple, carefully scooping out the flesh and keeping the shells. Discard the hard central core and cut the flesh into small pieces. Make the dressing: mix all the ingredients together and toss the pineapple and cherries in it. Chill for 1 hour. Add the gammon and pile into the pineapple shells. Garnish with the chopped walnuts and decorate with watercress.

Orange honey ham salad

1 Danish gammon joint
300ml/½ pint orange juice
1 onion
1 bay leaf
30ml/2 tablespoons honey
15ml/1 tablespoon Demerara sugar
Garnish:
2 large oranges
2 kiwi fruit, peeled and sliced

Soak the gammon joint for a few hours, drain and place in a pan with 175ml/6floz orange juice and sufficient water to cover. Add the onion and bay leaf. Bring to the boil and then simmer for 25 minutes to every 450g/1lb plus 10 minutes. Remove the rind. Mix the honey and remaining orange juice together. Press the sugar onto the fat, pour the honey mixture over the joint and place in a baking tin. Cook in a moderate oven for 15 minutes. Cool thoroughly. Slice the ham thinly and arrange in the centre of a large serving dish. Peel the oranges and cut into rings. Arrange round the edge of the dish topped with slices of kiwi fruit.

Cheese, ham and pineapple salad

225g/8oz diced cooked ham
100g/4oz diced cheese, eg. red Leicester
225g/8oz large black and white grapes
1 peeled and sliced fresh pineapple, cut in chunks
50g/2oz beansprouts
150ml/¼ pint mayonnaise
30ml/2 tablespoons pineapple juice
salt and pepper

Arrange the ham, cheese, fruit and beansprouts on 4 plates. Blend the mayonnaise, pineapple juice and seasoning and put a spoonful on each plate. Garnish with pineapple leaves.

Raised meat pie

225g/8oz green bacon, cubed
350g/12oz breast of chicken, cubed
350g/12oz veal or pork, cubed
1 very small onion, finely chopped
salt and pepper
2.5ml/½ teaspoon mixed dried herbs
good pinch of nutmeg
2 medium eggs, hard-boiled and shelled
beaten egg for glazing
Hot-water crust pastry:
100g/4oz lard or white vegetable fat
150ml/¼ pint water
350g/12oz plain flour
2.5ml/½ teaspoon salt

Make the pastry: melt the lard and water and bring to the boil. Pour on to the flour and salt and knead to a soft dough. Roll out three-quarters to line a pie tin or 15cm/6in loose-bottomed cake tin and cover the remaining pastry with a damp cloth. Mix the meats, onion, seasoning, herbs and nutmeg and pack half into the tin. Lay the eggs side by side on top and cover with the remaining filling. Roll out the pastry to make a lid. Seal the edges. Brush with egg. Decorate with pastry leaves and make a hole in the top. Cook in a preheated oven at 200°C, 400°F, gas 6 for 30 minutes, covered with foil, then 1¼ hours at 170°C, 325°F, gas 3. Cool and serve. Fill with gelatine stock if wished.

Hot chicken and spinach salad

175g/6oz young spinach leaves, washed
6 spring onions, roughly chopped
30ml/2 tablespoons chopped hazelnuts
3 courgettes, thinly sliced
2 chicken breasts, skinned and boned
100ml/4floz olive or sunflower oil
1 onion, finely chopped
1 clove garlic, crushed
30ml/2 tablespoons white wine vinegar
salt and pepper
15ml/1 tablespoon chopped fresh tarragon
1 red pepper, seeded and thinly sliced

Tear the spinach into pieces and mix with the spring onion, nuts and courgette in a bowl. Cut the chicken into strips and fry briskly in 90ml/6 tablespoons of the oil with the onion and garlic until tender. Add the remaining oil, vinegar, seasoning and tarragon. Cook over high heat for 1 minute. Gently toss the spinach and chicken mixtures together with the red pepper. Serve hot.

Avocado chicken salad

350g/12oz cooked chicken, cut in chunks
16 black grapes, halved and seeded
1 radicchio
few sprigs watercress
½ avocado pear, peeled and thinly sliced
Dressing:
100ml/4floz natural yoghurt
60ml/4 tablespoons mayonnaise
2 avocado pears, stoned and peeled
juice of ½ lemon
salt and pepper
1 clove garlic, crushed (optional)

Make the dressing: blend the yoghurt and mayonnaise. Mash the avocado and mix with the lemon juice. Fold into the mayonnaise mixture and season to taste. Add crushed garlic if wished. Fold the chicken into the dressing with some of the grapes. Arrange on a dish garnished with radicchio and watercress topped with the remaining grapes and thinly sliced avocado.

Greek chicken salad

350g/12oz diced cooked chicken
8 cherry tomatoes, skinned
1 cucumber, cut in chunks
1 green pepper, seeded and chopped
100g/4oz black olives, stoned
3 spring onions, chopped
100ml/4floz vinaigrette dressing
juice of ½ lemon
15ml/1 tablespoon chopped oregano
15ml/1 tablespoon chopped mint

Place the chicken, vegetables and olives in a bowl and toss in the vinaigrette dressing and lemon juice. Sprinkle with herbs and serve with crusty bread.

Chicken and egg salad

225g/8oz cooked chicken
225g/8oz cooked long-grain rice
10ml/2 teaspoons turmeric
30ml/2 tablespoons tomato chutney
4 hard-boiled eggs, shelled
60ml/4 tablespoons green mayonnaise
cress or watercress to garnish
Dressing:
15ml/1 tablespoon tarragon vinegar
1.25ml/¼ teaspoon paprika
salt and pepper
dash of tabasco sauce
15ml/1 tablespoon tomato sauce
45ml/3 tablespoons oil

Dice the chicken and set aside. Colour the cooked rice with turmeric, forking it through gently, and place in a bowl. Make the dressing: put all the ingredients in a sealed container and shake well. Check the seasoning and mix into the rice. Place in a serving dish and stir in the chutney. Spread the chicken over the top. Cut the eggs into quarters and arrange around the chicken. Cover with the mayonnaise and garnish with cress. Serve with hot French bread or wholemeal rolls.

Chicken tonnato

4 boned and skinned chicken breasts
1 onion, halved
1 carrot, halved
1 bay leaf
sprigs thyme and parsley
salt and pepper
75g/3oz canned tuna
100ml/4floz mayonnaise
juice of $\frac{1}{2}$ lemon
15ml/1 tablespoon chopped capers
15ml/1 tablespoon crushed green peppercorns
100ml/4floz natural yoghurt
1 red pepper
4 black olives, stoned and halved
$\frac{1}{2}$ lemon, thinly sliced
curly endive and radicchio to garnish

Put the chicken in a pan and cover with water. Add the onion, carrot, herbs and seasoning. Bring to the boil and then simmer for about 20-30 minutes until cooked. Cool and drain. Slice the chicken breasts diagonally and overlap them down the centre of a serving dish. Blend or process the tuna, mayonnaise, lemon juice, capers, peppercorns and seasoning to a smooth paste. Thin with the yoghurt. Pour the tonnato sauce down the centre of the chicken. Grill the red pepper to char the skin. Peel, seed and cut into thin strips. Decorate with red pepper, olives and lemon. Garnish with curly endive and radicchio.

Exotic duck salad

1 roasted 2kg/4lb duckling
2 red dessert apples, cored and diced
50g/2oz chopped walnuts
2 kiwi fruit, peeled and sliced
2 heads chicory, separated into leaves
1 bunch watercress, washed and trimmed

Dressing:
60ml/4 tablespoons mayonnaise
5ml/1 teaspoon chopped capers
15ml/1 tablespoon chopped sweet and sour gherkins
10ml/2 teaspoons made mustard
15ml/1 tablespoon chopped parsley
juice of $\frac{1}{2}$ lemon

Strip the skin off the duckling and cook under a hot grill until really crisp and golden brown. Remove the duckling meat from the bones and cut into small chunks. Mix with the apple and walnuts in a bowl. Blend all the dressing ingredients together and toss the duckling salad gently. Place in the centre of a large plate and arrange the sliced kiwi fruit, chicons of chicory and sprigs of watercress in an attractive border around the edge. Crumble the crisp duck skin over the top.

Chinese chicken salad

$\frac{1}{2}$ cucumber, shredded
5 spring onions, shredded
1 green pepper, seeded and sliced
2 sticks celery, sliced diagonally
25g/1oz root ginger, shredded
100g/4oz cooked beansprouts
350g/12oz cooked chicken, shredded
45ml/3 tablespoons sesame oil
15ml/1 tablespoon soy sauce
5ml/1 teaspoon chilli sauce
5ml/1 teaspoon sugar
salt and pepper
15g/$\frac{1}{2}$oz sesame seeds

Mix the cucumber, onion, pepper, celery, ginger, bean-sprouts and chicken in a bowl. Blend the oil, soy and chilli sauces, sugar and seasoning and toss the chicken salad gently. Sprinkle with sesame seeds and leave for at least 30 minutes before serving.

Eastern chicken salad

350g/12oz cooked chicken, cut in chunks
50g/2oz cashew nuts, toasted
1 red pepper
1 yellow pepper
100g/4oz mange-tout
30ml/2 tablespoons sesame seeds
100ml/4floz oriental dressing
salt and pepper

Put the chicken and cashew nuts in a large bowl. Grill the peppers until charred and remove the outer skin and seeds. Chop the flesh roughly and add to the chicken mixture. Top, tail and string the mange-tout and blanch in boiling salted water for 1 minute. Drain and mix with the chicken mixture and sesame seeds. Toss lightly in the dressing. Season to taste.

Salmagundy

few lettuce leaves
1 large tomato, sliced
175g/6oz thin French beans
100g/4oz ham and tongue, cut in strips
7-8 slices cooked chicken breast
$\frac{1}{2}$ cucumber, thinly sliced
2 gherkins, cut in fans
1 hard-boiled egg, chopped
few leaves curly endive
175g/6oz canned red salmon and tuna, diced
few anchovy fillets, cut in slivers
90ml/6 tablespoons yoghurt salad dressing
15ml/1 tablespoon chopped chives

Arrange the lettuce leaves on a large serving plate. Place the sliced tomato in a pile on the edge and cook the beans until tender. Arrange in two bundles on either side of the tomato. Criss-cross the ham and tongue on either side of the beans and then arrange the chicken and cucumber in overlapping slices to fill the remaining space. Decorate with gherkin fans (see page 29) and chopped hard-boiled egg. Place a smaller plate on a pedestal in the centre of the dish and fill with the curly endive. Mix the salmon, tuna and anchovies into the yoghurt salad dressing and pile into the centre. Sprinkle with chives.

Fruity chicken salad

450g/1lb cooked chicken, diced
225g/8oz raspberries
175g/6oz cooked thin French beans
150ml/¼ pint Roquefort dressing
1 iceberg lettuce
30ml/2 tablespoons chopped chives

Put the chicken and raspberries in a bowl. Cut the French beans in half and fold carefully into the chicken mixture. Toss very gently in the Roquefort dressing so as not to damage the raspberries. Arrange on a bed of really crisp iceberg lettuce and sprinkle with chives.

Caribbean curried chicken

450g/1lb shredded, cooked chicken
6 slices pineapple, chopped
25g/1oz raisins
1 crisp lettuce
30ml/2 tablespoons shredded coconut
30ml/2 tablespoons mango chutney
75g/3oz peanuts
100ml/4floz natural yoghurt
45ml/3 tablespoons mayonnaise
5ml/1 teaspoon hot curry powder
30ml/2 tablespoons chopped parsley

Mix the chicken and pineapple and arrange on top of the lettuce. Pile the raisins, coconut, chutney and peanuts on top. Blend the yoghurt, mayonnaise and curry powder and spoon over the salad. Sprinkle with chopped parsley.

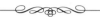

Summer chicken fruit salad

350g/12oz cooked chicken, shredded
16 strawberries, hulled
1 small pineapple, peeled and cubed
2 kiwi fruit, peeled and sliced
1 large mango, peeled and diced
50ml/2floz mayonnaise
100ml/4floz natural yoghurt
juice of 1 orange
30ml/2 tablespoons chopped chives

Arrange the chicken and fruit around the edge of a shallow dish or serving plate. Blend the mayonnaise, yoghurt and orange juice. Mix in the chives and pour into a small bowl. Stand in the middle of the dish.

Melon chicken salad

1 large cantaloup melon
1 avocado, peeled, stoned and diced
juice of 1 lemon
1 green pepper, seeded and diced
4 spring onions, chopped
50g/2oz raisins
225g/8oz cooked chicken, diced
100g/4oz cooked long-grain brown rice
30ml/2 tablespoons chopped fresh coriander or mint
100ml/4floz natural yoghurt
salt and pepper

Cut the top off the melon in a zig-zag pattern round the sides. Remove the seeds and scoop out the melon with a melon baller. Mix the melon with the avocado and lemon juice. Add the pepper, spring onion, raisins, chicken, rice and mint. Toss gently in the yoghurt, season to taste and pile into the hollowed-out melon.

Black cherry and duck salad

225g/8oz stoned black cherries
350g/12oz cooked duck, diced
45ml/3 tablespoons chopped chives
1 red pepper, seeded and diced
100ml/4floz green mayonnaise
1 curly endive
4 hard-boiled eggs, shelled and quartered

Fold the cherries, duck, chives and red pepper into the green mayonnaise. Arrange the curly endive in a bowl and pile the duck and cherry mixture into the middle. Garnish with the quartered eggs.

Devilled turkey salad

350g/12oz diced, cooked turkey
100g/4oz cooked thin French beans
1 large mango, peeled and cubed
2 peaches, stoned and cubed

50g/2oz toasted almonds
150ml/¼ pint sunflower oil
1 egg yolk
5ml/1 teaspoon tomato ketchup
15ml/1 tablespoon Worcestershire sauce
5ml/1 teaspoon grated lemon rind
salt and pepper
mint leaves to garnish
30ml/2 tablespoons chopped chives

Mix the turkey, beans, fruit and almonds together. Pour the oil into the egg yolk in a thin trickle, whisking all the time until the sauce thickens. Blend with the ketchup, Worcestershire sauce, lemon rind and seasoning to taste. Toss the chicken, fruit and nuts lightly in the devilled sauce and garnish with mint and chives.

Kidney bean and sausage salad

225g/8oz kidney beans
2 onions, chopped
1 large clove garlic, crushed
45ml/3 tablespoons oil
10ml/2 teaspoons sweet paprika
5ml/1 teaspoon hot paprika
225g/8oz garlic sausage, cubed
50ml/2floz natural yoghurt
50ml/2floz soured cream
15ml/1 tablespoon lemon juice
salt and pepper
30ml/2 tablespoons chopped parsley

Soak the kidney beans overnight and drain. Place in a pan with fresh water, bring to the boil and boil for 10 minutes. Drain the beans and refresh under running water. Replace in the pan with more fresh water and bring to the boil, reduce the heat and simmer for 1 hour or until tender. Drain. Sauté the chopped onion and garlic in the oil until soft and golden. Add the paprika and cook gently for 2 minutes. Mix the beans and onion mixture with the garlic sausage in a serving dish. Blend the yoghurt, soured cream and lemon juice and toss the bean salad in this dressing. Season to taste and sprinkle with plenty of chopped parsley.

Pasta, shrimp and avocado salad

2 avocados, peeled, stoned and cubed
225g/8oz peeled shrimps
juice of 1 lemon
350g/12oz cooked pasta shells
30ml/2 tablespoons chopped parsley
60ml/4 tablespoons olive oil
15ml/1 tablespoon wine vinegar
1 clove garlic, crushed
salt and pepper

Marinate the avocado and shrimps in lemon juice and mix with the pasta and parsley. Mix the oil and vinegar and add the garlic and seasoning. Gently toss the salad.

Citrus rice mould

350g/12oz cooked long-grain American rice
salt and pepper
1 bunch spring onions, washed and chopped
1 green pepper, seeded and finely diced
1 small bunch parsley, chopped
50ml/2floz mayonnaise
2 oranges, peeled and segmented
2 grapefruit, peeled and segmented
1 head chicory, separated into leaves
1 small bunch watercress, trimmed

Prepare the rice and mix with the seasoning, spring onion, green pepper, parsley and mayonnaise. Pile into a lightly oiled large ring mould (about 20cm/8in diameter) and chill for 2 hours until firm. Gently invert the ring mould on a large platter and turn out carefully without dislodging any grains of rice. Arrange the orange and grapefruit segments in an overlapping ring around the edge of the plate. Stand the chicory leaves in the centre with a few sprigs of watercress and serve.

Moroccan couscous salad

350g/12oz cold cooked couscous
60ml/4 tablespoons olive oil
½ cucumber, diced
1 clove garlic, crushed
3 tomatoes, skinned and chopped
6 spring onions, chopped
1 green pepper, seeded and chopped
225g/8oz cold cooked chicken, diced
1 red chilli, seeded and chopped
juice of 2 lemons
salt and pepper
30ml/2 tablespoons chopped mint
30ml/2 tablespoons chopped coriander

Mix the couscous and olive oil to remove any lumps and prevent sticking. Gradually add the cucumber, garlic, tomato, onion and pepper. Stir in the chicken, chilli and lemon juice. Season to taste. Mix with the herbs, saving a spoonful to sprinkle on top.

Salade du Midi

1 onion, finely chopped
1 leek, thinly sliced
45ml/3 tablespoons oil
450g/1lb tomatoes, skinned and chopped
pinch of sugar
2 cloves garlic, crushed
salt and pepper
225g/8oz thin French beans
juice of ½ lemon
4 hard-boiled eggs, shelled and quartered
8 artichoke hearts
8 black olives, stoned
1 small can anchovy fillets
30ml/2 tablespoons chopped parsley

Sauté the onion and leek in the oil until soft. Add the tomato, sugar, garlic and seasoning. Cook gently until the mixture thickens. Meanwhile, top and tail the beans and cook in boiling salted water until just tender but still slightly crisp. Drain and stir into the tomato mixture

with the lemon juice. Cool and arrange on a dish within a border of egg and artichoke hearts. Decorate with olives and a lattice of anchovies. Top with parsley.

Chick peas Italienne

175g/6oz chick peas
1 large onion, chopped
1 clove garlic, crushed
45ml/3 tablespoons olive oil
7.5ml/½ tablespoon tomato paste
450g/1lb canned or fresh tomatoes, skinned and chopped
5ml/1 teaspoon brown sugar
good pinch each powdered saffron and cinnamon
2.5ml/½ teaspoon oregano or basil
salt and pepper
30ml/2 tablespoons chopped parsley

Soak the chick peas overnight. Drain and cook in plenty of water for about 2 hours, or until tender. Drain and set aside. Sauté the onion and garlic in the oil until soft and translucent. Stir in the tomato paste and chopped tomato, the sugar, spices and herbs. Bring to the boil and cook until the sauce reduces and thickens. Season to taste and mix with the cooked chick peas. Leave to cool to room temperature and sprinkle with parsley.

Peasant salad

225g/8oz chick peas, soaked overnight
1 onion, finely chopped
1 clove garlic, crushed
1 red pepper, seeded and cut in rings
2 bunches watercress or a crisp lettuce, shredded
225g/8oz feta cheese, diced
2 hard-boiled eggs, quartered
4 tomatoes, skinned and quartered
Dressing:
60ml/4 tablespoons oil
30ml/2 tablespoons lemon juice
15ml/1 tablespoon chopped parsley or basil
salt and pepper

Cook the chick peas in the soaking water, adding more water if necessary to cover. Bring to the boil, and then simmer for 1½ hours, or until just tender. Do not over-cook. Drain and chill. Add the onion and garlic. Fold in the pepper and mix well. Make the dressing and pour two-thirds over the salad mixture. Toss together and chill for 1 hour. Wash the watercress and arrange on a serving platter with the chick pea mixture. Garnish with the feta cheese, egg and tomato. Sprinkle any remaining dressing over the top.

Wild rice salad

175g/6oz wild rice
350g/12oz cooked turkey, shredded
50g/2oz chopped walnuts
4 spring onions, chopped
1 green pepper, seeded and chopped
2 oranges, segmented
8 black olives, stoned
75ml/3floz vinaigrette dressing
45ml/3 tablespoons chopped parsley

Wash the wild rice in a sieve and then tip into a large pan of boiling salted water. Simmer with the pan covered for about 30 minutes, or until the rice is cooked. Drain and cool. Mix with the turkey, nuts, onion, pepper, orange and olives. Toss in the vinaigrette dressing and sprinkle with chopped parsley.

Prawn and rice salad

1 onion, finely chopped
5oz/2oz butter
100g/4oz long-grain rice
300ml/½ pint stock
50g/2oz button mushrooms, sliced
1 small can sweetcorn kernels
175g/6oz peeled prawns
15ml/1 tablespoon chopped parsley
6 spring onions, sliced
2 tomatoes, sliced

Dressing:
60ml/4 tablespoons oil
30ml/2 tablespoons tarragon vinegar
5ml/1 teaspoon sugar
2.5ml/½ teaspoon mustard
salt and pepper

Sauté the onion in the butter for 2-3 minutes. Add the rice and stir to thoroughly coat with oil. Cook for ½ minute. Add the stock and the mushrooms. Cover and cook for 12-15 minutes, or until the rice is just tender. Do not over-cook – all the liquid should be absorbed. Add the sweetcorn and the prawns. Fold in the parsley and spring onions. Make the dressing and fold into the salad gently. Check the seasoning and leave to cool. Place in a serving dish and garnish with sliced tomato.

Italian seafood rice salad

1kg/2lb mussels
225g/8oz long-grain Arborio rice
salt and pepper
juice of ½ lemon
75ml/3floz olive oil
4 anchovy fillets, chopped
45ml/3 tablespoons chopped parsley
8 cooked king prawns, shelled
225g/8oz cooked monkfish or any firm white fish
12 black olives, stoned

Scrub the mussels and wash well to remove any mud and grit. Throw away any open or gaping ones. Put them in a deep saucepan with a little water and bring to the boil. Cover the pan and cook for a few minutes, shaking occasionally. Discard any mussels that do not open. Shell most of the open mussels but reserve a few in their blue-black shells for decoration. Cook the rice in boiling salted water until tender. Drain and rinse under running cold water. Mix with the seasoning, lemon juice, oil, anchovy and parsley. Fold in the shelled mussels and prawns. Cut the fish into chunks and mix into the rice with the olives. Garnish with the reserved mussels.

Layered party rice

225g/8oz long-grain American rice
10ml/2 teaspoons turmeric
salt and pepper
60ml/4 tablespoons vinaigrette dressing
1 small cos lettuce, shredded
4 large carrots, grated
3 red apples, cored and diced
juice of 1 small lemon
2 small green peppers, seeded and chopped
3 oranges, peeled and sliced
30ml/2 tablespoons chopped chives

Cook the rice, drain well and fork in the turmeric until it is evenly golden. Season and add the vinaigrette. Spread half the rice over the base of a *glass* serving dish. Top with a layer of shredded lettuce and then one of grated carrot. Cover with the remaining rice and then a layer of apple (soaked in lemon juice to prevent discolouration). Cover with green pepper and arrange the sliced oranges on top. Sprinkle with chopped chives.

Fruit and nut rice salad

225g/8oz long-grain American rice
60ml/4 tablespoons vinaigrette dressing
15ml/1 tablespoon lemon juice
2 red apples, cored and diced
2 pineapple rings, diced (or canned in natural juice)
2 peaches, diced (or canned in natural juice)
75g/3oz raisins
75g/3oz walnuts, chopped
50g/2oz peanuts, chopped
salt and pepper
1 small crisp lettuce, eg. Webb's
60ml/4 tablespoons natural yoghurt

Cook the rice, drain well and toss in the vinaigrette dressing while still hot. Set aside to cool. Pour the lemon juice over the apple. Add the pineapple, peaches, raisins and nuts. Mix in the rice and season with salt and pepper. Serve on a bed of crisp lettuce. Dribble the yoghurt over the top and serve.

Main courses

Cooking rice in the Multi Server

You can cook perfect fluffy rice in Tupperware's Multi Server.

1 Fill the outer bowl of the Multi Server three-quarters full with water and pour into a saucepan with a good pinch of salt. Bring to the boil.

2 Add 250ml white rice and stir. Bring to the boil and cook for 5 minutes.

3 Pour the rice and water into the inner bowl of the Multi Server, cover and leave for 20 minutes.

4 Lift out the inner colander to drain the rice. Pour away the starchy water. When the rice is cool, flavour or colour as wished. Add the chopped or shredded ingredients of your choice and serve as a rice salad in the Multi Server itself.

Spanish prawn salad

350g/12oz long-grain rice
juice of ½ lemon
100ml/4floz olive oil
salt and pepper
30ml/2 tablespoons chopped parsley
4 spring onions, chopped
2 tomatoes, skinned, seeded and chopped
1 red pepper, seeded and chopped
350g/12oz peeled cooked prawns

Cook the rice until tender. Rinse under running cold water. Mix with the lemon juice, oil and seasoning until every grain is glistening. When cool, mix in the remaining ingredients and serve.

Spanakoriso salad

1kg/2lb spinach, washed and trimmed
2 large onions, chopped
75ml/3floz green olive oil
225g/8oz long-grain rice
400ml/15floz hot water
salt and pepper
juice of ½ lemon
chopped fresh oregano

Cook the spinach in a little salted water for about 5 minutes until tender. Drain and cool, squeezing out the moisture. Sauté the onion in the oil until soft and translucent. Chop the spinach and add to the pan with the rice. Stir well until all the grains are glistening with oil. Add the hot water and bring to the boil. Reduce the heat to a simmer, cover the pan and cook gently until the rice is cooked and tender, and all the liquid absorbed. Season well and cool. Stir in the lemon juice and chopped herbs and serve at room temperature.

Genovese pasta salad

225g/8oz pasta spirals
50g/2oz fresh basil leaves
few sprigs parsley
50g/2oz pine nuts
1 clove garlic, crushed
25g/1oz grated Parmesan cheese
juice of ½ lemon
75ml/3floz olive oil
100ml/4floz yoghurt salad dressing
30ml/2 tablespoons mayonnaise
salt and pepper
2 tomatoes, quartered
2 hard-boiled eggs, quartered
few basil leaves

Cook the pasta spirals until *al dente*. Meanwhile, put the herbs, most of the pine nuts, garlic, Parmesan and lemon juice in a blender or food processor. Process to a paste. Add the oil in a trickle and process until thick. Season to taste. Mix with the dressing. Drain the pasta, cool and toss in the sauce. When cold, serve with the tomatoes and eggs. Sprinkle with the remaining pine nuts and basil leaves.

Mediterranean rice salad

225g/8oz long-grain rice
salt and pepper
75ml/3floz lemon vinaigrette dressing
1 red pepper
1 green pepper
4 spring onions, chopped
2 tomatoes, skinned and cut in wedges
8 black olives, stoned
30ml/2 tablespoons chopped parsley

Cook the rice until tender. Rinse under cold running water and drain. Season well and toss lightly in the dressing. Grill the peppers until blistered. Cool and skin. Remove the seeds and cut into thin strips. Mix into the rice with the onion, tomato and olives. Sprinkle with plenty of parsley.

Italian sausage pasta salad

275g/10oz cooked pasta twists
1 red pepper, seeded and diced
175g/6oz garlic sausage, diced
50g/2oz peperami, sliced
12 black olives, stoned
4 spring onions, chopped
30ml/2 tablespoons chopped parsley and chives
90ml/6 tablespoons lemon vinaigrette
1 red oak-leaf lettuce

Mix the pasta, pepper, garlic sausage, peperami, olives, onions and herbs in a bowl. Toss in the dressing. Arrange on a bed of lettuce.

Curried rice salad

350g/12oz cooked long-grain American rice
2 dessert apples, cored and chopped
30ml/2 tablespoons lemon juice
450g/1lb diced cooked chicken
1 green pepper, seeded and chopped
45ml/3 tablespoons peanuts
100ml/4floz natural yoghurt
5ml/1 teaspoon mild curry powder
45ml/3 tablespoons seedless raisins

Mix the cooked rice and apples in the lemon juice. Add the chicken, pepper and peanuts. Blend the yoghurt, curry powder and raisins and toss the salad.

Salmon and pasta salad

350g/12oz freshly made linguine or tagliatelle
225g/8oz fresh salmon, skinned and boned
100g/4oz smoked salmon, cut in strips
225g/8oz shelled cooked prawns
60ml/4 tablespoons olive oil
juice of $\frac{1}{2}$ lemon
salt and pepper
45ml/3 tablespoons chopped parsley and tarragon

Cook the pasta in boiling salted water until tender (about 2-3 minutes). Drain and mix in a little oil to prevent the strands sticking together. Cut the salmon into large chunks and lightly poach or steam. Mix with the pasta, smoked salmon and prawns. Blend the oil, lemon and seasoning and gently toss the salad in the dressing. Sprinkle with herbs.

Pasta primavera

225g/8oz pasta spirals
2 small courgettes, thinly sliced
175g/6oz salami, diced
60ml/4 tablespoons sesame oil
salt and pepper
few coriander seeds, crushed
30ml/2 tablespoons chopped oregano
nasturtium flowers to garnish (optional)

Cook the pasta spirals until slightly tender but not soft. Drain and mix with the courgettes, salami and oil. Season to taste and add the coriander seeds and oregano. Leave to cool and garnish with nasturtium flowers.

Ligurian pasta salad

450g/1lb canned tomatoes
salt and pepper
pinch sugar
few basil leaves
1 clove garlic, crushed
1 can anchovies, chopped
8 green olives, stoned
350g/12oz prawns, shelled
450g/1lb penne
150ml/¼ pint olive oil

Purée the tomatoes, seasoning, sugar, basil and garlic. Mix with the anchovies, olives and prawns. Cook the penne in boiling salted water until tender but not soft. Drain and toss lightly in the olive oil before it cools. Mix with the tomato mixture and serve at room temperature.

Macaroni vegetable salad

350g/12oz cold cooked wholewheat macaroni
225g/8oz mozzarella, diced
2 slim courgettes, thinly sliced
3 tomatoes, skinned, seeded and roughly chopped
3 spring onions, chopped
100g/4oz stoned black olives
100ml/4floz vinaigrette dressing
45ml/3 tablespoons chopped parsley

Mix the cooked macaroni, mozzarella cheese, courgette, tomato, onion and olives in a bowl. Toss in the vinaigrette dressing and serve sprinkled with parsley.

Seafood pasta salad

225g/8oz pasta shells
100ml/4floz vinaigrette dressing
juice of $\frac{1}{2}$ lemon
30ml/2 tablespoons chopped chives
350g/12oz cod or fresh haddock
150ml/$\frac{1}{4}$ pint dry white wine
salt and pepper
225g/8oz peeled prawns
225g/8oz smoked salmon (or smoked mackerel fillets)
1 green pepper, seeded and diced
15ml/1 tablespoon chopped dill
100g/4oz cooked prawns in shells

Cook the pasta until tender. Drain, cool and season. Place in a large serving dish. Mix the dressing and lemon juice and pour 30ml/2 tablespoons over the pasta with the chives. Skin and bone the cod or haddock, cut into small pieces and place in a pan with the wine and seasoning. Bring to the boil and simmer for 2-3 minutes, adding the prawns for the last minute. Remove the fish and allow to cool Boil the fish liquid down to reduce to 15ml/1 tablespoon. Cool and pour over the pasta. Cut the salmon into strips about 5cm/2in long and 2.5cm/1in wide, reserving a few pieces for the garnish. Add the remainder with the cooked fish to the pasta. Fold in the chopped pepper and dill. Chill for 2 hours. Garnish with the reserved salmon and the unshelled prawns.

Chicken pasta salad

225g/8oz pasta shells
225g/8oz cooked chicken, diced
225g/8oz seedless grapes
50g/2oz blue cheese, cubed
75g/3oz toasted hazelnuts
150ml/5floz natural yoghurt
45ml/3 tablespoons mayonnaise
juice of $\frac{1}{2}$ lemon
salt and pepper
45ml/3 tablespoons chopped chives

Cook the pasta shells in boiling salted water until tender. Drain, rinse in cold water and cool. Mix with the chicken, grapes, blue cheese and nuts in a large bowl. Blend the yoghurt, mayonnaise, lemon juice and seasoning to make the dressing and toss the salad. Sprinkle with chives.

Spicy pasta salad

1 small onion, finely chopped
45ml/3 tablespoons dry white wine
5ml/1 teaspoon curry powder
90ml/6 tablespoons mayonnaise
5ml/1 teaspoon lemon juice
salt and pepper
350g/12oz freshly cooked pasta spirals
350g/12oz Lucanica Italian sausage
1 red pepper, seeded and sliced
10ml/2 teaspoons chopped parsley
8 black olives

Simmer the onion in the wine until tender. Add the curry powder and cook for 1 minute. Set aside. Blend the mayonnaise with the lemon juice and seasoning to taste. Cook the pasta and toss with the onion mixture. Leave until cool. Stir in the mayonnaise. If the mixture is too thick, add some more lemon juice or a little yoghurt. Grill the sausage, cut into slices, cool and fold into the salad. Place in a serving dish and garnish with the pepper. Sprinkle with parsley and olives.

A salad can be served as an accompaniment to the main dish or even afterwards to refresh the palate. The recipes on the following pages are light and delicious, and make an excellent foil to most meat, fish, pasta and rice dishes. You can serve a simple tossed green salad or a more exotic mixture of colourful beans or oranges and peppers. Instead of serving boiled, creamed or baked potatoes, try a warm potato salad tossed in vinaigrette with herbs.

These colourful side salads will complement any main course: Waldorf salad (opposite), Italian zucchini salad (below left) and Oriental salad (below). The recipes are on page 84.

Mixed green salad

lettuce: Cos, Webbs, Iceberg, Romaine
green peppers, seeded and sliced
cucumber, sliced or diced
spring onions, either whole or chopped
watercress, washed
chives, chopped
cooked French beans, whole or sliced
raw broad beans, choose only young ones
spinach, stems removed and washed
mange-tout, trimmed
young garden peas
chopped celery
curly endive
chicory
Chinese leaves
Garnish:
green olives, sunflower seeds, sliced kiwi fruits
vinaigrette dressing

Mixed green salads vary according to the season and what salad leaves you have at your disposal. Above are suggestions for ingredients that can be tossed together in a mixed salad. Try to choose salad stuffs of contrasting greens and textures for added interest and 'bite'. A vinaigrette is the usual dressing.

Waldorf salad

4 large red dessert apples
juice of 1 large lemon
4 sticks celery
60ml/4 tablespoons chopped walnuts
100ml/4floz mayonnaise mixed with yoghurt
salt and pepper
few lettuce leaves

Cut the apples into quarters and remove the cores, leaving the peel intact. Dice and sprinkle with lemon juice to prevent discolouration. Chop the celery and toss with the walnuts in the mayonnaise and yoghurt dressing. Season and arrange on a bed of lettuce leaves.

Italian zucchini salad

4 baby courgettes (zucchini), thinly sliced
350g/12oz tomatoes, thinly sliced
3 spring onions, thinly sliced
30ml/2 tablespoons chopped oregano
12 black olives
Dressing:
75ml/3floz olive oil
15ml/1 tablespoon tarragon vinegar
5ml/1 teaspoon Dijon mustard
pinch sugar
salt and pepper
squeeze lemon juice

Put all the dressing ingredients in a sealed container and shake well. Toss all the salad vegetables, herbs and olives gently in the dressing and serve.

Oriental salad

225g/8oz beansprouts and alfalfa
4 spring onions, chopped
2 carrots, grated
1 bunch watercress
60ml/4 tablespoons olive oil
20ml/4 teaspoons tamari sauce
juice of 1 lemon
15ml/1 tablespoon honey
a little grated fresh or pinch ground ginger

Mix the beansprouts, onion, carrot and watercress. Blend the dressing ingredients and gently toss the salad. Serve to accompany stir-fried Chinese dishes.

Mediterranean tomato salad

6 tomatoes, peeled and sliced
1 cucumber, peeled and diced
1 green pepper, seeded and sliced
25g/1oz pine nuts
15ml/1 tablespoon chopped parsley

Dressing:
45ml/3 tablespoons oil
30ml/2 tablespoons lemon juice
salt and sugar to taste
5ml/1 teaspoon chopped mint

Place the tomatoes, cucumber and pepper in a serving bowl. Mix the dressing and pour over the tomato mixture. Chill. Just before serving add the nuts and parsley.

Simple tomato salad

450g/1lb ripe tomatoes, peeled and thinly sliced
5ml/1 teaspoon sugar
60ml/4 tablespoons oil
45ml/3 tablespoons orange juice
1 clove garlic, crushed
grated lemon rind
salt and black pepper
15ml/1 tablespoon chopped basil, oregano or chives

Place the tomatoes in a serving dish and sprinkle with sugar. Mix the oil, orange juice, garlic, lemon rind and seasoning. Pour over the tomatoes and garnish with the herbs. Chill for 30 minutes before serving. This is excellent with grilled fish, barbecued steak or pizza.

Kyrenia salad

1 cucumber, diced
4 oranges, segmented
4 tomatoes, peeled and sliced
5ml/1 teaspoon grated orange rind
30ml/2 tablespoons chopped oregano
Dressing:
150ml/¼ pint plain yoghurt
150ml/¼ pint soured cream
½ clove garlic, crushed
10ml/2 teaspoons sugar
good pinch salt
30ml/2 tablespoons chopped mint
30ml/2 tablespoons lemon juice

Mix the dressing in a bowl and add the cucumber and orange segments. Mix well and chill for 30 minutes. Place the sliced tomatoes in a serving dish and pour over the dressing mixture. Garnish with the grated orange rind and chopped oregano.

North African salad

4 tomatoes, skinned and chopped
1 green pepper, seeded and chopped
1 red pepper, seeded and chopped
1 chilli pepper, seeded and chopped
5 spring onions, chopped
1 clove garlic, crushed
30ml/2 tablespoons chopped mint
15ml/1 tablespoon chopped parsley
50ml/2floz olive oil
juice of ½ lemon
salt and pepper
½ cucumber, chopped

Mix the tomato, peppers, chilli, onion, garlic and herbs in a bowl. Blend the oil, lemon and seasoning. Toss the salad and chill. Stir in the cucumber and serve.

Cotswold salad

2 slices wholemeal toast
12 small tomatoes, peeled and sliced
5ml/1 teaspoon caster sugar
1 large cucumber, thinly sliced
1 bunch spring onions, thinly sliced
salt and pepper
60ml/4 tablespoons vinaigrette dressing
225g/8oz curd cheese
15ml/1 tablespoon chopped chives
few radishes, sliced

Place the toast in the base of a serving dish. Cover with a layer of tomatoes, sprinkled with a little of the sugar. Add a layer of cucumber and then the onions. Lightly season. Repeat the layers until all the ingredients are used. Pour the dressing over the salad and top with the cheese. Garnish with chives and radishes. Serve with garlic rolls or crusty bread.

Peach salad

275g/10oz canned peaches in natural juice, drained
2 avocados, stoned, peeled and sliced
15ml/1 tablespoon lemon juice
6 firm tomatoes, peeled and sliced
2.5ml/$\frac{1}{2}$ teaspoon ground cumin
2.5ml/$\frac{1}{2}$ teaspoon ground coriander
5ml/1 teaspoon honey
45ml/3 tablespoons vinaigrette dressing
5ml/1 teaspoon Worcestershire sauce
100g/4oz blue cheese, sliced
10ml/2 teaspoons chopped tarragon and basil

Place the peaches and avocado in a dish and pour the lemon juice over the top. Mix the tomatoes with the spices. Make the dressing, adding the honey and Worcestershire sauce. Neatly arrange the peaches and avocado with the cheese on top of the tomatoes and cover with the dressing. Scatter with herbs.

Spinach salad

225g/8oz spinach
100g/4oz mushrooms, sliced
2 spring onions, finely chopped
60ml/4 tablespoons vinaigrette dressing
100g/4oz blue cheese, cubed
4 bacon rashers, grilled and crumbled

Wash the spinach well. Remove the stems and pat dry. Place in a salad bowl. Add the sliced mushroom and spring onion. Toss the salad in the dressing. Garnish with the blue cheese and crumbled bacon.

Banana salad

3 large unripe bananas, sliced
juice of ½ orange or lemon
½ cucumber, sliced
1 small green chilli, finely chopped
25g/1oz cashew nuts (or salted peanuts)
300ml/½ pint natural yoghurt
10ml/2 teaspoons chopped mint
salt and pepper
1 bunch watercress, washed

Slice the bananas and leave to stand in the juice. Add the cucumber and chilli, stir well, and mix in the nuts. Mix the yoghurt with the mint, season to taste and pour over the salad. Garnish with the watercress.

Italian-style beetroot salad

450g/1lb boiled beetroot, sliced
1 small onion, thinly sliced
60ml/4 tablespoons vinaigrette dressing
30ml/2 tablespoons chopped mint

Arrange the sliced beetroot and onion on a dish. Pour over the vinaigrette and sprinkle with fresh mint.

Beetroot and orange salad

1 small jar cooked beetroot
1 curly endive, shredded
2 oranges, segmented
1 onion, cut into thin rings
1 green pepper, thinly sliced
90ml/6 tablespoons vinaigrette dressing
30ml/2 tablespoons orange juice
grated rind of 1 orange
1 clove garlic, crushed

Slice the beetroot and drain well. Place the endive in a serving dish with the sliced beetroot in the centre. Arrange the orange segments in a fan around the edge. Garnish with the onion and pepper. Mix the vinaigrette with the orange juice and rind and garlic. Pour over the salad. Serve with cold meats or cheese.

Beetroot fantasy

75g/3oz raisins
30ml/2 tablespoons orange juice
4 small beetroot, grated
1 small can unsweetened pineapple, chopped
10ml/2 teaspoons chopped basil
10ml/2 teaspoons chopped mint
175ml/6floz natural yoghurt
salt and pepper
25g/1oz chopped walnuts

Marinate the raisins in the orange juice for 1 hour. Mix the beetroot with the pineapple and add the raisins. Fold the herbs into the yoghurt and season. Toss the salad gently and garnish with walnuts.

Norwegian beetroot salad

450g/1lb boiled beetroot, diced
2 apples, cored and diced
225g/8oz cooked waxy potatoes, diced
4 rollmop herrings, cut in strips
2 hard-boiled eggs, sliced
1 red onion, cut in rings
30ml/2 tablespoons chopped dill
creamy dressing:
175ml/6floz thick soured cream
5ml/1 teaspoon white wine vinegar
5ml/1 teaspoon mustard
good pinch of sugar
salt and pepper

Mix the beetroot, apple and potato in a dish. Blend all the ingredients for the dressing and gently toss the beetroot mixture. Garnish with rollmop herring strips, egg and onion and sprinkle with plenty of chopped dill.

Cheesy carrot pâté salad

4 large carrots, grated
100g/4oz cream or curd cheese
1 clove garlic, crushed
juice of ½ lime
salt and pepper
few coriander seeds, crushed
30ml/2 tablespoons chopped chives
30ml/2 tablespoons thick natural yoghurt
2 clementines, peeled and segmented
1 bunch watercress, washed and trimmed

Mix the grated carrot, cheese, garlic, lime juice, seasoning, coriander, chives and yoghurt in a bowl until well blended to a smooth pâté. Pile into the centre of a serving dish and arrange the clementines and watercress in a pretty border around the edge.

Carrot and raisin salad

350g/12oz grated carrot
100g/4oz California raisins
45ml/3 tablespoons soured cream or natural yoghurt
30ml/2 tablespoons chopped hazelnuts
salt and pepper
chives or chopped parsley

Put the carrot and raisins in a bowl. Blend the soured cream with the hazelnuts and season. Mix into the salad and sprinkle with herbs.

Carrot, date and raisin salad

4 large carrots, grated
50g/2oz dates
50g/2oz raisins
25g/1oz walnuts
300ml/½ pint natural yoghurt
5ml/1 teaspoon chopped mint
grated rind and juice of 1 lime
salt and pepper

Place the grated carrot in a dish. Stone the dates, cut in half and add with the raisins to the carrot. Lightly chop the walnuts and add to the salad. Fold in the yoghurt, mint and lime rind and juice. Season to taste. This is excellent with cold ham or pork.

Greek carrot salad

450g/1lb carrots
100ml/4floz green olive oil
juice of 1 large lemon
2 spring onions, finely chopped
1 clove garlic, crushed
salt and pepper
5ml/1 teaspoon chopped oregano
2.5ml/½ teaspoon chopped mint
pinch sugar

Peel or scrape the carrots, cut into thin strips and cook in boiling water until just tender but still a little crisp. Mix the remaining ingredients to make a dressing and gently toss the drained carrots. Serve slightly warm.

Chick pea salad

75g/3oz raisins
30ml/2 tablespoons dry white wine
2 red peppers, seeded and diced
1 onion, chopped
15ml/1 tablespoon chopped mixed herbs
350g/12oz cooked or canned chick peas
75ml/3floz vinaigrette dressing
30ml/2 tablespoons lemon juice
2.5ml/½ teaspoon chopped root ginger
salt and pepper
few sprigs watercress
30ml/2 tablespoons chopped parsley

Soak the raisins in the wine for two hours. Mix with the pepper, onion, herbs and chick peas. Add the dressing, lemon juice and ginger and season to taste. Chill and serve garnished with watercress and chopped parsley.

Three bean salad

450g/1lb can kidney beans

450g/1lb can chick peas

100g/4oz cooked thin French beans, halved

3 spring onions, finely chopped

75ml/3floz vinaigrette dressing

juice of $\frac{1}{2}$ lemon

salt and pepper

Drain and rinse the kidney beans and chick peas and mix with the French beans. Add the chopped onion, dressing and lemon juice. Season to taste.

Mexican bean salad

450g/1lb cooked kidney beans
1 red pepper, cut in rings
1 green pepper, cut in rings
1 large onion, cut in rings
chopped chives and parsley
75ml/5 tablespoons olive oil
juice of ½ lemon
good dash wine or herb vinegar
salt and pepper

Put the beans, pepper rings, onion and herbs in a bowl. Mix the remaining dressing ingredients together and toss the salad gently.

Curly endive with kiwi fruit

1 curly endive, shredded
3 spring onions, finely chopped
60ml/4 tablespoons vinaigrette dressing
15ml/1 tablespoon chopped parsley
½ cucumber, sliced
4 kiwi fruits, peeled and sliced

Mix the endive and onions and toss in the vinaigrette dressing and parsley. Arrange the sliced cucumber and kiwi fruit over the top.

Fennel salad

2 bulbs fennel, trimmed and finely sliced
1 green pepper, seeded and sliced
2 sticks celery, finely chopped
2 red dessert apples, cored and sliced
15ml/1 tablespoon lemon juice
½ cucumber, diced
150ml/¼ pint mayonnaise
30ml/2 tablespoons orange juice
30ml/2 tablespoons natural yoghurt
3 hard-boiled eggs, quartered
30ml/2 tablespoons chopped parsley

Place the fennel, pepper and celery in a serving dish. Mix the apples with the lemon juice and add to the fennel with the cucumber. Thin the mayonnaise with the orange juice and yoghurt and fold into the salad. Garnish with the eggs and parsley.

Chicory and nut peach salad

4 heads chicory, washed and quartered
1 bunch watercress, washed
4 peaches, peeled and sliced or halved
100g/4oz roughly chopped mixed nuts
100ml/4floz Roquefort dressing

Prepare the chicory and watercress. Arrange the watercress on a serving plate with the chicory and peaches on top. Scatter with nuts and coat with the dressing.

Curly endive and orange salad

1 curly endive, shredded (use lettuce if unavailable)
3 oranges, segmented
30ml/2 tablespoons chopped chives
15ml/1 tablespoon chopped basil or parsley
300ml/½ pint natural yoghurt
30ml/2 tablespoons orange juice
5ml/1 teaspoon grated orange rind
black pepper
12 black olives
garlic croûtons

Prepare the curly endive and leave in the refrigerator for 30 minutes to crisp up. Add the oranges and sprinkle with the herbs. Mix the yoghurt with the orange juice and rind, add pepper to taste and serve with the salad. Garnish with olives and garlic croûtons.

California salad

1 crisp lettuce
100g/4oz grated carrot
1 red and 1 green pepper, chopped
1 stick celery, chopped
2 courgettes/zucchini, sliced
2 small tomatoes, quartered
salt and pepper
1 avocado, stoned and peeled
100ml/4floz French dressing
1 clove garlic, crushed

Put the salad vegetables in a bowl with the seasoning. Mash the avocado flesh to a purée. Blend with the French dressing and garlic and toss the salad.

Courgette and pepper salad

450g/1lb courgettes, thinly sliced
6 spring onions, thinly sliced
1 green pepper, seeded and thinly sliced
1 green chilli, seeded and finely chopped

Dressing:
60ml/4 tablespoons oil
15ml/1 tablespoon chopped fresh mint
15ml/1 tablespoon lemon juice
30ml/2 tablespoons cider vinegar
10ml/2 teaspoons honey
salt and pepper

Mix the courgette, onion, pepper and chilli together. Place all the dressing ingredients in a sealed container and shake well. Pour over the salad and chill for 2 hours. Serve with pasta, cold meat or cheese.

Courgette and potato salad

450g/1lb cooked potatoes, cut into chunks
450g/1lb courgettes, sliced and blanched for 2 minutes
juice and grated rind of 1 lemon
150ml/$\frac{1}{4}$ pint mayonnaise
30ml/2 tablespoons natural yoghurt
salt and pepper
15ml/1 tablespoon chopped mint
100g/4oz crisp-grilled bacon rashers

While the potatoes are cooling blanch the courgettes in salted water, drain and cool. Mix with the lemon juice and grated rind. Blend the mayonnaise and yoghurt, adding seasoning if necessary. Add the mint, and fold carefully into the courgettes and potatoes. Crumble the bacon over the top of the salad.

Beetroot and butter bean salad

400g/14oz canned butter beans
6 carrots, grated
350g/12oz sliced cooked beetroot in vinegar
10ml/2 teaspoons chopped chives
Dressing:
60ml/4 tablespoons oil
15ml/1 tablespoon wine vinegar
30ml/2 tablespoons orange or lemon juice
1 clove garlic, crushed

Drain the butter beans and make the dressing. Toss the beans in half of the dressing and arrange in the centre of a large serving dish. Use the carrot round the edge to form a border, pouring the remaining dressing over the top. Arrange the beetroot in overlapping slices round the dish. Garnish with chives.

Turkish bitter-sweet salad

3 large seedless oranges
few crisp lettuce leaves
1 Spanish onion, thinly sliced
5ml/1 teaspoon coriander seeds, crushed
45ml/3 tablespoons good olive oil
2.5ml/½ teaspoon paprika
salt and pepper
75g/3oz black olives, stoned

Peel the oranges and thinly slice in circles. Place in a serving dish on top of the lettuce with the onion. Sprinkle with coriander. Blend the oil and paprika and pour over the top. Season to taste. Mix in the olives. Chill.

Side salads

Italian fennel salad

2 fennel bulbs
4 spring onions, chopped
1 can anchovy fillets
3 tomatoes, quartered
½ cucumber, sliced
225g/8oz ricotta cheese
50ml/2floz olive oil
15ml/1 tablespoon herb vinegar
juice of 1 lemon
good pinch sugar
salt and pepper
few slivers lemon peel
30ml/2 tablespoons chopped parsley

Slice the fennel thinly, and mix with the onion, anchovies, tomato, cucumber and ricotta. Blend the oil, vinegar and lemon juice with the sugar and seasoning and gently toss the salad. Top with thin slivers of lemon peel and parsley.

Italian fennel and tomato salad

350g/12oz tomatoes, skinned and sliced
2 fennel bulbs, sliced
salt and pepper
pinch sugar
few basil leaves
60ml/4 tablespoons olive oil
15ml/1 tablespoon lemon juice
dash red wine vinegar

Arrange the tomato and fennel in overlapping circles on a dish. Season and sprinkle the tomato with sugar. Garnish with basil leaves. Mix the oil, lemon juice and vinegar and pour over the salad.

Green bean salad

450g/1lb thin French beans, trimmed and sliced
60ml/4 tablespoons vinaigrette dressing
10ml/2 teaspoons Dijon mustard

Cook the prepared beans in salted water for 4-5 minutes. Drain, refresh and dry. Place in a serving dish. Blend the dressing and mustard and pour over the beans. Add a chopped green chilli if wished

Provençale leek salad

1kg/2lb leeks
30ml/2 tablespoons olive oil
350g/12oz tomatoes
juice of 1 lemon
pinch sugar
salt and pepper
30ml/2 tablespoons chopped parsley
8 stoned black olives

Clean the leeks and cut into 2.5cm/1in lengths. Sweat in the oil over low heat until tender. Remove the leeks. Skin and chop the tomatoes and add to the pan with the lemon juice, sugar and seasoning. Cook gently for 10-15 minutes. Leave to cool, pour over the leeks and serve garnished with parsley and olives.

Mushroom salad

175g/6oz button mushrooms
15ml/1 tablespoon oil
1 small onion, finely chopped
60ml/4 tablespoons red wine
60ml/4 tablespoons vinaigrette dressing
salt and pepper
15ml/1 tablespoon chopped basil or chives
5ml/1 teaspoon dried or chopped dill

Wash the mushrooms. Heat the oil in a pan and sauté the onion gently for 2-3 minutes. Add the mushrooms and sauté for 2 minutes. Remove and add the red wine to the pan. Boil hard to reduce to half the original volume. Pour over the mushrooms with the vinaigrette dressing and season to taste. Garnish with the herbs. Chill well.

Raw mushroom salad

225g/8oz button mushrooms
2 cloves garlic, crushed
15ml/1 tablespoon chopped parsley
juice of 1 lemon
30ml/2 tablespoons oil
salt and pepper
50g/2oz green olives
sprinkling paprika

Wipe the mushrooms and thinly slice into a bowl. Mix the garlic, parsley and lemon juice with the oil and season to taste. Stone the olives. Toss the mushrooms and olives in the dressing and chill for 2 hours. Sprinkle with paprika just before serving.

Avocado nut salad

2 avocado pears, peeled, stoned and sliced
2 small red dessert apples
juice of 1 small lemon
60ml/4 tablespoons cashew nuts
100ml/4floz natural yoghurt
good pinch curry powder
30ml/2 tablespoons chopped oregano
1 bunch watercress

Place the avocado in a bowl. Core and dice the apples and add to the bowl. Sprinkle with lemon juice. Add the nuts, yoghurt, curry powder and herbs and toss gently. Arrange on a bed of watercress.

Four nut salad

100g/4oz walnuts, roughly chopped
75g/3oz almonds, blanched and cut into slithers
50g/2oz pine nuts
100g/4oz seedless raisins
100g/4oz dates, stoned
3 spring onions, thinly sliced
12 apricots, stoned and halved

15ml/1 tablespoon chopped chives
salt and pepper
175ml/6floz green yoghurt dressing
sprinkling paprika
25g/1oz chopped pistachio nuts

Place all the ingredients except the dressing, paprika and pistachio nuts in a serving dish. Mix well and fold in the dressing. Sprinkle with paprika and pistachios.

Spanish onion salad

2 large Spanish onions, thinly sliced
1 red pepper, seeded and thinly sliced
1 green chilli, finely chopped
15ml/1 tablespoon chopped parsley
Dressing:
30ml/2 tablespoons oil
15ml/1 tablespoon lemon juice
2.5ml/½ teaspoon Dijon mustard
salt and pepper
2.5ml/½ teaspoon ground coriander

Place the onion, pepper and chilli in a dish. Mix the dressing and pour over the salad. Leave in the refrigerator, covered, to chill for 1 hour. Sprinkle with parsley.

Orange and pepper salad

2 green peppers, seeded and sliced in rings
4 spring onions, chopped
4 large oranges, peeled and sliced
1 curly endive
45ml/3 tablespoons olive oil
juice of 1 orange
1 clove garlic, crushed
salt and pepper
45ml/3 tablespoons chopped chives

Mix the pepper, onion, orange and endive. Blend the oil, orange juice, garlic and seasoning to make a tangy dressing. Toss the salad and sprinkle with chives.

Crunchy apple and cauliflower salad

1 small cauliflower, divided into florets
3 sticks celery, chopped
2 small red dessert apples, cored and diced
100g/4oz peanuts
150ml/¼ pint natural yoghurt
juice of 1 orange
30ml/2 tablespoons chopped parsley

Mix the cauliflower, celery, apple and peanuts together in a bowl. Blend the yoghurt and orange juice and season. Toss the salad gently and sprinkle with parsley.

Cucumber and dill salad

3 cucumbers, thinly sliced
salt
few sprigs dill to garnish
150ml/¼ pint soured cream
30ml/2 tablespoons sunflower oil
15ml/1 tablespoon white wine vinegar
2.5ml/½ teaspoon sugar
freshly ground black pepper
30ml/2 tablespoons chopped fresh dill

Sprinkle the cucumber with salt and leave for 1 hour to exude any juice. Rinse under running cold water and pat dry. Arrange the cucumber in overlapping concentric circles on a large serving dish and garnish with sprigs of dill. Blend the cream, oil, vinegar and sugar. Season to taste and mix in the chopped dill. Chill well and serve separately in another dish.

99

Pineapple and cheese salad

1 pineapple or 1 large can unsweetened pineapple
10ml/2 teaspoons soft brown sugar
15ml/1 tablespoon chopped chives
$\frac{1}{2}$ red pepper, seeded and chopped
150ml/$\frac{1}{4}$ pint vinaigrette dressing
1 crisp lettuce, shredded
225g/8oz ricotta or curd cheese
15ml/1 tablespoon chopped parsley

Peel and core the pineapple and cut into small pieces. Add the sugar and chives with the chopped pepper. Toss in the vinaigrette dressing and stand for 30 minutes. Prepare the lettuce and chill for 30 minutes to crisp it up. Place in a serving dish and pile the pineapple mixture on top. Place the cheese in a mound in the centre and garnish with parsley.

New potato salad

450g/1lb new potatoes, cooked in their skins
4 rashers grilled bacon
4 spring onions, chopped
150ml/$\frac{1}{4}$ pint natural yoghurt
juice of $\frac{1}{2}$ lemon
30ml/2 tablespoons chopped parsley
45ml/3 tablespoons mayonnaise
salt and pepper
45ml/3 tablespoons chopped chives

Cut the potatoes into small chunks and place in a bowl with the crumbled bacon and onion. Mix the yoghurt, lemon juice, parsley and seasoning, and toss the salad gently. Sprinkle with chives.

Potatoes vinaigrette

450g/1lb new potatoes
1 bunch spring onions, chopped
15ml/1 tablespoon chopped parsley
150ml/$\frac{1}{4}$pint vinaigrette dressing
175g/6oz crisp-grilled bacon, crumbled

Cook the potatoes in boiling salted water, preferably in their skins. Cut into small pieces and, while still warm, mix with the onions, parsley and dressing. Put aside to cool. Crumble the bacon over the potatoes.

Radish, orange and watercress salad

4 large oranges
1 bunch watercress
1 bunch radishes, sliced
150ml/$\frac{1}{4}$ pint natural yoghurt
good pinch ground cinnamon
45ml/3 tablespoons chopped chives

Peel the orange, removing the white pith and slice thinly crossways. Mix in a bowl with the watercress and radishes. Blend the yoghurt, cinnamon and any leftover orange juice and spoon over the salad. Sprinkle with chives.

Quick rice salad

350g/12oz cooked American long-grain rice
1 small can sweetcorn kernels
1 red pepper, seeded and chopped
60ml/4 tablespoons vinaigrette dressing
3 small tomatoes, quartered
$\frac{1}{2}$ cucumber, sliced

Mix the rice, sweetcorn, peppers and the dressing. Garnish with tomato and cucumber.

Rice and pimento salad

225g/8oz long-grain brown rice
60ml/4 tablespoons vinaigrette dressing
2 red peppers
1 green pepper, seeded and chopped
salt and black pepper
8 black olives, halved

Cook the rice in boiling salted water until tender but still firm. Drain and rinse. Fold in the dressing and cool.

Grill the red peppers and remove the charred skins. Remove the seeds and cut one into dice, the other into slices. Add the chopped peppers and season to taste. Garnish with the rings of red pepper placing a halved olive in each ring.

Minty rice salad

350g/12oz cooked American long-grain rice
100g/4oz cooked peas
100g/4oz chopped celery
3 spring onions, chopped
15ml/1 tablespoon chopped fresh mint
100ml/4floz natural yoghurt
black pepper

Mix together the rice and vegetables. Blend the mint, yoghurt and seasoning and toss with the rice salad.

Watercress salad

2 bunches watercress, washed
100g/4oz button mushrooms, sliced
30ml/2 tablespoons chopped fennel
1 avocado, peeled, stoned and sliced
juice of $\frac{1}{2}$ lemon
1 grapefruit, segmented
15ml/1 tablespoon chopped chives
Dressing:
15ml/1 tablespoon lemon juice
2.5ml/$\frac{1}{2}$ teaspoon Dijon mustard
1 clove garlic, crushed
15ml/1 tablespoon grapefruit juice
5ml/1 teaspoon sugar
salt and pepper
45ml/3 tablespoons oil

Place the watercress, mushroom and fennel in a dish. Prepare the avocado and brush with lemon juice. Prepare the grapefruit, reserving 15ml/1 tablespoon of the juice for the dressing. Mix all the ingredients together and toss in the dressing.

Orange and watercress salad

2 bunches watercress
2 large oranges, peeled and sliced
3 spring onions, chopped
12 black olives
45ml/3 tablespoons toasted flaked almonds
50ml/2floz sunflower oil
juice of 2 oranges

Pick over the watercress and wash well. Place in a salad bowl with the orange, onion, olives and almonds. Blend the oil and orange juice and toss the salad gently.

Peach and watercress salad

4 fresh peaches or nectarines
60ml/4 tablespoons Roquefort or vinaigrette dressing
2 bunches watercress
toasted almonds

Slice the peaches and marinate in the chosen dressing for 30 minutes. Place the watercress on a serving dish with the peaches arranged in the centre. Scatter with almonds. Serve with ham, pork, bacon or cheese.

Elizabethan herb salad

mixed salad leaves eg. corn salad, purslane, rocket, salad burnet, sorrel
fresh herbs eg. tarragon, chervil, parsley
60ml/4 tablespoons green olive oil
30ml/2 tablespoons Seville orange juice
5ml/1 teaspoon Tewkesbury mustard
salt and pepper
pinch sugar

Trim and wash the salad leaves and herbs. Spin dry. Mix the oil, orange juice, mustard, seasoning and sugar and toss the salad until every leaf is glistening. Decorate if wished with edible flowers.

Just because winter has arrived and the days are shorter, greyer and colder, there is no reason to stop eating fresh salads. You can make some sensational winter salads with seasonal root vegetables, imported exotic fruit and winter salad leaves such as chicory and lamb's lettuce. Red cabbage, radicchio, grated carrot, winter spinach and Chinese leaves can create a colourful, nutritious salad to accompany a hot main course. And seasonal nuts, lychees, apples and grapefruit all add interest, flavour and texture to a salad.

Winter salads can be very versatile and vividly coloured. Here are Fruit cabbage salad (opposite), Belgian winter salad (below left) and Red winter salad (below). The recipes are all on page 104.

Winter salads

Red winter salad

1 head radicchio
1 red-oakleaf lettuce
225g/8oz red cabbage, shredded
1 small red-skinned onion, finely chopped
350g/12oz cooked or canned red kidney beans
50g/2oz halved walnuts
6 rashers streaky bacon, chopped
few fried bread croutons
Dressing:
45ml/3 tablespoons walnut or virgin olive oil
10ml/2 teaspoons tarragon vinegar
salt and pepper
5ml/1 teaspoon Dijon mustard

Wash and spin dry the radicchio and lettuce and arrange with the cabbage in a bowl. Add the onion, kidney beans and walnuts. Cook the bacon in its own fat until golden and crisp. Mix the dressing and gently toss the salad. Top with the bacon and croûtons.

German winter salad

225g/8oz cooked chicken, diced
100g/4oz cooked ham, diced
1 pickled herring fillet, chopped
225g/8oz cooked potatoes, diced
1 red onion, finely chopped
2 red dessert apples, cored and diced
juice of ½ lemon
4 sweet gherkins, chopped
50g/2oz chopped walnuts
100ml/4floz soured cream
100ml/4floz mayonnaise
salt and pepper
2 hard-boiled eggs, shelled and quartered
15ml/1 tablespoon chopped parsley

Mix the chicken, ham, herring, potato and onion in a bowl. Brush the apple with lemon juice and stir into the mixture with the gherkins and nuts. Blend the soured cream and mayonnaise. Season to taste and fold into the salad. Chill well and garnish with egg and parsley.

Fruit cabbage salad

350g/12oz shredded white cabbage
75g/3oz chopped dried apricots
100g/4oz California raisins
4 spring onions, chopped
1 small green pepper, seeded and chopped
Dressing:
100ml/4floz natural yoghurt
2.5ml/½ teaspoon French mustard
1 clove garlic, crushed
salt and pepper
squeeze lemon juice

Gently mix all the salad ingredients together in a large bowl. Blend the yoghurt with the other dressing ingredients and toss the salad lightly.

Belgian winter salad

2 heads chicory, sliced
50g/2oz walnuts, roughly chopped
100g/4oz thinly sliced smoked ham (Parma or Bayonne)
60ml/4 tablespoons vinaigrette dressing
30ml/2 tablespoons chopped parsley

Prepare the chicory and mix with the walnuts. Cut the ham into small pieces and add to the salad. Toss in the vinaigrette dressing and sprinkle with chopped parsley.

Lebanese tabbouleh

225g/8oz burghul (cracked wheat)
300ml/½ pint water
60ml/4 tablespoons chopped fresh mint
5 spring onions, finely chopped
1 bunch parsley, finely chopped
juice of 1 lemon
30ml/2 tablespoons olive oil
salt and pepper

5 cabbage leaves
½ red pepper, seeded and thinly sliced
6 black olives
¼ cucumber, thinly sliced

Soak the burghul in the water for 30 minutes until it soaks up the liquid and expands. Mix with the mint, onion, parsley, lemon juice, oil and seasoning to taste. Arrange a bed of cabbage leaves on a large plate and pile the tabbouleh into a pyramid shape in the centre. Decorate the sides with the sliced red pepper, olives and cucumber.

Dutch coleslaw

225g/8oz Dutch hard white cabbage
3 crisp dessert apples, cored and diced
45ml/3 tablespoons lemon juice
1 small onion, grated or finely chopped
1 red pepper, diced
450g/1lb Dutch cheese (Edam or Gouda), diced
1 bunch watercress
Dressing:
5ml/1 teaspoon mustard
60ml/4 tablespoons mayonnaise
10ml/2 teaspoons sugar
15ml/1 tablespoon apple juice
15ml/1 tablespoon chopped parsley

Grate the cabbage into a large bowl. Brush the apples with the lemon juice and mix with the onion, red pepper and cabbage. Make the dressing and fold into the salad. Chill for 1 hour. Add the cheese and garnish with sprigs of watercress.

Avocado winter salad

2 avocados, peeled, stoned and sliced
few crisp lettuce leaves
few sprigs watercress
1 small onion, thinly sliced
1 small red pepper, sliced
2 tomatoes, quartered or sliced
50ml/2floz vinaigrette dressing

Mix the salad ingredients together and toss well in the dressing. Serve immediately. If wished, use Chinese leaves instead of lettuce for a more crunchy texture.

Avocado and raisin salad

2 avocados, peeled, stoned and thinly sliced
30ml/2 tablespoons lemon juice
100g/4oz raisins
3 carrots, coarsely grated
4 spring onions, chopped
45ml/3 tablespoons olive oil
juice of 1 orange
salt and pepper
few chopped chives

Sprinkle the avocado with lemon juice to prevent discolouration. Mix with the raisins, carrot and onion. Blend the oil and orange juice, season and gently toss the salad. Sprinkle with a mist of chives.

Beetroot and pineapple salad

2 cooked beetroot, finely grated
1 small pineapple, peeled, cored and chopped
3 sticks celery, chopped
350g/12oz blue brie or blue cream cheese
25g/1oz cashews or walnuts
Dressing:
15ml/1 tablespoon pineapple juice
15ml/1 tablespoon lemon juice
15ml/1 tablespoon oil
5ml/1 teaspoon chopped parsley
salt and pepper

Mix the beetroot, pineapple and celery in a bowl. Make the dressing and pour over the top. Chill for 1 hour. Pile the cheese in the centre of a serving plate or dish and arrange the dressed salad ingredients round the edge. Scatter the nuts over the top.

Pasta fruit salad

225g/8oz cooked pasta shells or rings
1 red dessert apple, cored and diced
3 small oranges, peeled and segmented
45ml/3 tablespoons walnuts, chopped
3 sticks celery, chopped
1 small bunch watercress
100ml/4floz natural yoghurt
juice of 1 orange

Mix the pasta, fruit, nuts, celery and watercress together. Blend the yoghurt and orange juice and toss the salad.

Curried pasta salad

350g/12oz cooked pasta shells
225g/8oz canned tuna chunks
4 spring onions, chopped
150ml/$\frac{1}{4}$ pint natural yoghurt
5ml/1 teaspoon mild curry powder
juice of $\frac{1}{2}$ lemon
45ml/3 tablespoons mayonnaise
45ml/3 tablespoons chopped parsley

Put the pasta, tuna and onion in a bowl. Mix the remaining dressing ingredients and toss well so that the pasta is well-coated. Sprinkle with parsley.

Winter salads

Spicy apple salad

100ml/4floz soured cream
5ml/1 teaspoon mustard
5ml/1 teaspoon sugar
5ml/1 teaspoon sweet paprika
2.5ml/½ teaspoon caraway seeds
salt and pepper
1 small Savoy cabbage, finely shredded
1 small red onion, chopped
3 red dessert apples, cored and sliced
juice of ½ lemon
30ml/2 tablespoons chopped parsley

Blend the soured cream, mustard, sugar, paprika, caraway seeds and seasoning. Mix with the cabbage and onion. Brush the apple with lemon juice and mix into the dressing. Serve sprinkled with parsley.

French red cabbage salad

1 red cabbage, shredded
few leaves curly endive or chicory
6 rashers crisp grilled bacon, crumbled
225g/8oz blue cheese, crumbled eg. Roquefort
crisp-fried bread croûtons
75ml/3floz olive oil
15ml/1 tablespoon tarragon vinegar
5ml/1 teaspoon Dijon mustard
pinch sugar
salt and pepper

Put the red cabbage, endive, bacon, cheese and croûtons in a salad bowl. Blend the remaining dressing ingredients and gently toss the salad.

Carrot and grapefruit salad

4 carrots, grated
2 grapefruit, segmented
3 heads chicory
30ml/2 tablespoons grapefruit juice

30ml/2 tablespoons oil
pinch sugar
salt and pepper
15ml/1 tablespoon chopped parsley
6 black olives, stoned

Place the grated carrot in a serving dish with the grapefruit segments, reserving any juice for the dressing. Trim the chicory, cut into quarters or slice and arrange around the grapefruit. Mix the grapefruit juice, oil, sugar and seasoning and toss the salad. Sprinkle with parsley and scatter with a few black olives. Serve with ham, soft cheese or winter casseroles.

Celeriac salad

675g/1½lb celeriac
juice of ½ lemon
175ml/6floz mayonnaise or soured cream
5ml/1 teaspoon horseradish relish or sauce
salt and pepper
25g/1oz chopped walnuts
30ml/2 tablespoons chopped parsley

Peel the celeriac and cut into thin julienne strips (about the size of a matchstick). Cook in boiling salted water with the lemon juice for 5 minutes. Drain and cool. Blend the mayonnaise or cream with the horseradish and fold into the celeriac. Season to taste. Scatter the nuts and parsley over the top and serve. This is an excellent accompaniment to cold roast beef.

Normandy celeriac salad

1 celeriac, peeled and grated coarsely
30ml/2 tablespoons white wine vinegar
2 Cox's apples, cored and thinly sliced
350g/12oz cold cooked turkey, diced
100ml/4floz vinaigrette dressing
30ml/2 tablespoons chopped parsley

Add the celeriac and vinegar to a pan of boiling water.

Bring back to the boil and then drain the celeriac. Pat dry and mix with the apple and turkey. Toss in a vinaigrette dressing. Sprinkle with parsley.

Chicken and chicory salad

350g/12oz cooked chicken, cut in strips
1 large head chicory, washed and sliced
1 radicchio, washed and separated in leaves (optional)
1 red dessert apple, cored and diced
100g/4oz Swiss cheese, diced
75g/3oz walnuts, chopped
1 bunch watercress, washed and trimmed
1 small red pepper, thinly sliced
30ml/2 tablespoons mayonnaise
100ml/4floz natural yoghurt
juice of ½ lemon
salt and pepper
15ml/1 tablespoon chopped parsley

Place the chicken, chicory, radicchio, apple, cheese, nuts, cress and red pepper in a bowl. Blend the mayonnaise, yoghurt and lemon juice. Season and toss the salad gently. Sprinkle with chopped parsley.

French bean and chicory salad

175g/6oz cold, cooked French beans
2 heads chicory, thinly sliced or shredded
15ml/1 tablespoon chopped chives or basil
2 oranges, segmented
Dressing:
60ml/4 tablespoons oil
1 clove garlic, crushed
60ml/4 tablespoons orange juice
salt and pepper

Make the dressing: place the ingredients in a sealed container and shake well. Place the beans and chicory in a serving dish and toss in the dressing. Add the herbs, mix well and garnish with the orange. This is a good winter salad served with hard cheese or cold meats.

Chicory and orange salad

3 heads chicory
1 bunch watercress, washed
30ml/2 tablespoons chopped chives
15ml/1 tablespoon chopped parsley
4 spring onions, chopped
30ml/2 tablespoons vinaigrette dressing
3 large oranges, segmented

Prepare the chicory and arrange in a dish with the watercress, chives, parsley, chopped onion and vinaigrette dressing. Arrange the orange segments on top. Serve with roast meat and poultry.

Chinese leaf salad

1 head Chinese leaves, sliced
1 onion, chopped
1 red pepper, seeded and sliced
1 fresh pineapple, peeled and chopped
50g/2oz chopped walnuts
1 bunch watercress
100ml/4floz natural yoghurt
2.5ml/½ teaspoon curry powder
juice of ½ lemon

Put the Chinese leaves, onion, pepper, pineapple, walnuts and watercress in a bowl. Blend the yoghurt, curry powder and lemon juice and gently toss the salad.

Jerusalem artichoke vinaigrette

450g/1lb Jerusalem artichokes
60ml/4 tablespoons vinaigrette dressing
juice of ½ lemon
3 spring onions, chopped
25g/1oz toasted hazelnuts, roughly chopped
30ml/2 tablespoons chopped parsley

Cook the Jerusalem artichokes in salted water until just tender. Peel away the skins and cut into chunks, removing any blemishes. Toss in the vinaigrette and lemon juice with the onion. Sprinkle with hazelnuts and parsley.

Red cabbage slaw

1 small red cabbage, shredded
4 sticks celery, chopped
4 carrots, grated
2 red dessert apples, cored and diced
15ml/1 tablespoon lemon juice
1 onion, grated
1 green pepper, seeded and chopped
50g/2oz raisins
good pinch of paprika
Dressing:
60ml/4 tablespoons oil
30ml/2 tablespoons cider vinegar
5ml/1 teaspoon Dijon mustard
5ml/1 teaspoon honey
salt and pepper

Place the cabbage, celery and carrot in a large dish. Brush the apple with lemon juice and add to the cabbage with the onion, pepper and raisins. Make the dressing: either mix well or place in a sealed container and shake. Season to taste. Fold into the cabbage mixture. Chill and sprinkle with a dusting of paprika.

Winter spinach salad

350g/12oz trimmed spinach
450g/1lb peeled prawns
50g/2oz toasted hazelnuts, roughly chopped
8 lychees, peeled and stoned
1 pomegranate, quartered
100ml/4floz vinaigrette dressing
30ml/2 tablespoons chopped parsley

Wash and dry the spinach. Arrange in a salad bowl with the prawns, nuts and lychees. Carefully remove the bright red seeds from the pomegranate and add to the salad. Toss gently in the vinaigrette dressing and sprinkle some chopped parsley over the top.

Christmas salad

1 heart Chinese leaves
3 carrots, grated
75g/3oz raisins, sultanas or seedless grapes
150ml/$\frac{1}{4}$pint vinaigrette dressing
225g/8oz chestnuts, cooked and peeled
1 can unsweetened pineapple slices
8 Maraschino cherries
15ml/1 tablespoon chopped parsley
1 bunch watercress
300ml/$\frac{1}{2}$pint acidulated cream dressing

Wash the Chinese leaves and place in the refrigerator to 'crisp up'. Mix the grated carrot with the dried fruit or grapes and vinaigrette dressing. Leave to stand for 15 minutes. Fold in the chestnuts. Place the Chinese leaves in a salad dish with the fruit mixture in the centre. Arrange the pineapple over the top, with a cherry in the centre of each slice. Sprinkle with the parsley and decorate the edge with watercress. Serve with the acidulated cream dressing with cold turkey or goose.

Spiced turkey salad

450g/1lb cold, cooked turkey
1 bunch spring onions, chopped
1 green pepper, seeded and diced
3 tomatoes, peeled and sliced
4 slices pineapple, diced
2 bananas, sliced
15ml/1 tablespoon lemon juice
1 lettuce or curly endive, shredded
30ml/2 tablespoons pineapple juice
12 black olives
25g/1oz toasted almonds
Dressing:
2 tomatoes, peeled
30ml/2 tablespoons chopped mint
30ml/2 tablespoons chopped parsley
2.5ml/$\frac{1}{2}$ teaspoon grated root ginger
1 onion, chopped
2.5ml/$\frac{1}{2}$ teaspoon ground coriander
1 small fresh chilli
250ml/8floz natural yoghurt
salt and pepper

Dice the turkey and prepare the dressing. Place the tomatoes, herbs, ginger, onion and spices in a liquidizer or food processor and blend together. Fold in the yoghurt and season to taste. Pour half the mixture over the turkey, onions, peppers and tomatoes with the pineapple and banana brushed with lemon juice and mix together. Shred the endive and spread over a serving platter. Sprinkle with pineapple juice. Place the turkey mixture in the centre and garnish with olives and almonds.

Leek salad

8 slim leeks
75ml/3floz vinaigrette dressing
juice of ½ lemon
8 black olives, stoned
1 hard-boiled egg, shelled and chopped
30ml/2 tablespoons chopped parsley

Clean and trim the leeks but do not slice them – leave whole. Cook in boiling salted water until just tender but still slightly crisp. Drain and arrange in a long serving dish. When cool, pour the vinaigrette and lemon juice over the top and chill well. Serve garnished with olives, egg and parsley.

Winter potato salad

450g/1lb potatoes, cooked
50g/2floz vinaigrette dressing
30ml/2 tablespoons chopped chives
90ml/6 tablespoons mayonnaise
175g/6oz button mushrooms
25g/1oz butter
freshly ground black pepper
15ml/1 tablespoon lemon juice
175g/6oz streaky bacon
15ml/1 tablespoon chopped parsley

Cut the potatoes into small chunks whilst warm and toss carefully in the vinaigrette dressing. Leave to cool. Add the chives to the mayonnaise and fold into the potatoes.

Cook the mushrooms quickly in the butter, remove and add lots of black pepper and sprinkle with lemon juice. Mix with the potatoes. Grill the bacon until crisp. Crumble over the salad with the parsley.

Hot dill potato salad

450g/1lb small or new potatoes
3 spring onions, chopped
10ml/2 teaspoons dried dill
few anchovy fillets
75ml/3floz natural yoghurt or soured cream
squeeze lemon juice
salt and pepper
chopped dill or chives to garnish

Boil the potatoes until tender but still firm. Cut into chunks and mix with the onion, dill and anchovies. Toss gently in the yoghurt and lemon juice. Season and sprinkle with herbs. Serve the salad while it is still warm.

Swiss walnut salad

100g/4oz Gruyère cheese, diced
1 red dessert apple, cored and sliced
2 spring onions, chopped
1 large bunch watercress
75g/3oz halved walnuts
3 hard-boiled eggs, shelled and quartered
45ml/3 tablespoons walnut oil
5ml/1 teaspoon red wine vinegar
2.5ml/½ teaspoon Dijon mustard
pinch of sugar
1 clove garlic, crushed
salt and pepper

Mix the cheese, apple and onion in a bowl. Wash and trim the watercress and add to the salad with the walnuts and egg. Blend the oil, vinegar, mustard, sugar, garlic and seasoning. Toss the salad in this dressing and serve.

Cheese and salad have a natural affinity. What could make a more delicious and simple lunch than an interesting cheese board surrounded by colourful salads? Cheese is often served with celery and garnished with lettuce leaves and sprigs of parsley. Most cheeses can be sliced or diced into salads, whether they are creamy, melting Bries, crumbly goat's cheese, sharp, hard Cheddars, soft herb cheeses or blue-veined Stilton.

Choosing cheese

Avoid the pre-packed cheeses sweating gently in their polythene wrappings. Always try to buy cheese cut fresh off a block when it is just ripe and ready to eat. Most cheese counters do not mind if you ask for a small 'taster' of an unfamiliar cheese before committing yourself.

When preparing a cheese board, choose cheeses of different colours, textures and shapes to add interest and delight your guests. If you enjoy the old favourites like Brie, Cheshire, Gouda and Stilton, serve them rubbing shoulders with more unusual cheeses like the Italian

Taleggio, the British Cornish Yarg, the French Tomme au raisin and the Swiss Vacherin. Try to strike some sort of balance between hard, soft and creamy, blue-veined, herb and peppercorn-flavoured varieties, and strong and mild cheeses. Garnish the cheese board with sticks of tender celery, a bunch of grapes or whole nuts.

Variety

There is no excuse nowadays for not experimenting with cheese. The counters of supermarkets and delicatessens are stacked with a fine array of cheeses from many countries. In fact, the choice is so overwhelming that many people just opt for a nice soft Cheddar or Brie.

There are even specialist cheese shops that cater for the growing interest in cheese, especially those cheeses that are made in the traditional way without additives. Some of the cheeses on sale in supermarkets tend to be mass-produced and soapy in texture, and there is a demand for naturally produced, properly aged cheese.

Cheeses may be made from cow's, goat's or sheep's milk and come in a wide range of shapes and colours – from blue-veined cheeses like Roquefort to red Leicester and green sage Derby. It may be very hard like the Italian Parmesan and Romano; hard like Cheddar and Emmenthal; semi-hard like Port-Salut and Stilton; soft like Camembert and Brie; or soft and runny like Vacherin.

Cheese storage

Although cheese needs to be stored at a constant cool temperature, it should never be over-chilled. Storage in the refrigerator can kill a good cheese, causing the rind and cut surfaces to dehydrate and a subsequent loss of flavour. A cool old-fashioned larder is best, preferably furnished with a marble slab on which cheeses wrapped in muslin can sit.

Of course, in hot weather or the absence of a larder, it may be necessary to store cheese in the refrigerator in which case protect it by sealing in a plastic container and store in the salad crisper compartment (the least cold part). If so, remove the cheese at least a couple of hours before serving to allow it to adapt to room temperature.

Cheese is a 'living' product and it is important that it should 'breathe' and that air be allowed to circulate freely around it. Hard cheeses can be wrapped in damp muslin to keep them suitably moist and prevent any tendency to dryness. Place a fine mesh cover over the cheese if possible.

English cheeses can make an attractive cheeseboard as illustrated opposite. There is a wide range of different colours, textures and flavours including blue-veined Stilton (1), traditional mature Cheddar (2), Welsh Caerphilly (3), sage Derby (4) and red Leicester (5). Cheese has a natural affinity with wine, which is its classical partner. A bunch of juicy grapes offsets the sharpness of the cheese and decorates the cheeseboard. Use either black or white.

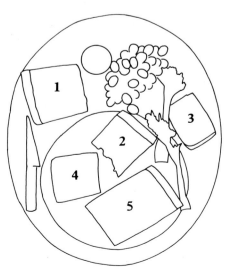

When storing cheese, wrap different cheeses separately. The flavours should never be allowed to mingle. A strong-smelling Ambassador or Gorgonzola can impair a more delicately flavoured cheese if stored together.

How long can you store cheese? Hard and semi-hard cheeses will keep well for several weeks if stored correctly, but most soft cheeses have a higher moisture content and keep less successfully. Runny, soft cheeses like Brie and Vacherin have a very short shelf life and should be consumed as soon as they ripen. Even storage in a refrigerator will not halt or slow down this ripening process so do not push them to the back and forget about them. Eat and enjoy them at their best.

Thick creamy and fresh cheeses like cottage cheese, ricotta, Petit Suisse, fromage frais and cream or curd cheeses should always be kept in a refrigerator and eaten within a few days of purchase. Look for a 'sell by' date on the carton when you buy it.

Serving cheese

Cheese can be eaten at any time of the day. The Germans like to serve it for breakfast, the Americans with cocktails in 'happy hour' while many people munch it as snacks throughout the day or even eat it with biscuits and pickles for a late supper (cheese is supposed to induce fanciful dreams if eaten at bedtime!). It can be served with soup, salad and fresh bread for a light lunch or as part of a formal dinner, usually between the main course and the dessert or at the end of the meal. There is no correct time to serve cheese and it is really up to you to decide when and how you wish to eat it.

Cheese in salads

Soft and crumbly cheeses can be blended into salad dressings as in the case of Roquefort dressing, or crumbled over a salad. Hard cheeses can be cubed or sliced and mixed into a fresh salad, whereas fromage frais can be used to toss a salad.

The recipes overleaf show just how versatile cheese can be in adding flavour, texture and colour. Remember also that cheese can transform a simple side salad into a main course by adding essential protein and vitamins. Many people are slimming-conscious nowadays and if you regard cheese as a high-fat food, you may prefer to eat the new low-fat cheeses, cottage cheese and quark. They can all be included in interesting salads, especially when mixed with chopped fresh seasonal fruit.

Stilton salad

225g/8oz Stilton, diced
4 sticks celery, sliced
1 small melon, peeled, seeded and thinly sliced
2 green peppers, seeded and sliced
60ml/4 tablespoons natural yoghurt
15ml/1 tablespoon mayonnaise
good squeeze lemon juice
1 head radicchio
30ml/2 tablespoons chopped chives

Mix the Stilton, celery, melon and pepper in a bowl. Blend the yoghurt and mayonnaise with the lemon juice and gently mix into the Stilton mixture. Arrange the radicchio on a dish and pile the Stilton salad .in the centre. Decorate with chives.

Stilton and watercress salad

2 bunches watercress
50g/2oz curly endive
100g/4oz Stilton cheese
50g/2oz halved walnuts
2 ripe pears, peeled, cored and thinly sliced
4 rashers streaky bacon
50ml/2floz vinaigrette dressing

Wash, dry and trim the watercress. Mix with the curly endive in a bowl. Crumble the Stilton cheese into the salad with the nuts and pears. Grill the bacon until crisp and crumble into the salad. Toss lightly in the dressing.

Cheesy tomato salad

4 large tomatoes
225g/8oz blue Brie
1 avocado, peeled, stoned and sliced
75ml/3floz vinaigrette dressing
4 basil leaves
freshly ground black pepper

Skin the tomatoes and slice thinly. Arrange on a serving

dish. Remove the rind from the cheese and cut into cubes. Arrange the avocado down the centre in overlapping slices and scatter the cubes at the sides. Dress with the vinaigrette. Place the basil leaves on top and sprinkle with plenty of black pepper.

Autumn Cheddar salad

225g/8oz Chinese leaves
1 bunch watercress
6 spring onions, sliced diagonally
225g/8oz farmhouse Cheddar cheese, cubed
4 red dessert apples, cored and sliced
50g/2oz halved green walnuts
100ml/4floz vinaigrette dressing
45ml/3 tablespoons chopped parsley

Wash the Chinese leaves and watercress and spin dry. Tear the leaves into pieces and trim the watercress. Put in a bowl with the spring onions, cheese, apple and nuts. Toss gently in the vinaigrette and sprinkle with plenty of chopped parsley.

Cheese and pasta salad

100g/4oz wholemeal pasta rings
45ml/3 tablespoons vinaigrette dressing
2 red apples, cored and thinly sliced
100g/4oz Cheddar cheese, diced
25g/1oz raisins
3 sticks celery, sliced
50g/2oz toasted hazelnuts
45ml/3 tablespoons soured cream
juice and grated rind of 1 orange
salt and pepper
30ml/2 tablespoons chopped parsley

Cook the pasta in boiling salted water until tender. Drain and toss in the vinaigrette dressing. Mix with the apple, cheese, raisins, celery and nuts. Blend the soured cream, orange juice and rind and season to taste. Mix into the salad and sprinkle with parsley.

Mozzarella and salami salad

450g/1lb large ripe tomatoes
2 Italian mozzarella cheeses
100g/4oz piece salami, cubed
8 anchovy fillets
8 black olives
75ml/3floz vinaigrette dressing
sprig fresh basil leaves

Quarter the tomatoes and cut the quarters in half again. Cut the mozzarella into large cubes. Mix the tomato and cheese with the salami, anchovies and olives in a bowl. Toss in the dressing and garnish with the basil leaves.

Fruity cheese and rice salad

225g/8oz brown rice
sea salt and pepper
2 cloves garlic, crushed
5ml/1 teaspoon coriander seeds, crushed
5ml/1 teaspoon chopped fresh oregano
225g/8oz thin French beans
100g/4oz toasted hazelnuts
1 pineapple, peeled, cored and cubed
100g/4oz peeled cooked prawns
150ml/5floz fromage frais
juice and grated rind of 2 oranges

Cook the rice in boiling salted water until tender. Drain and season with sea salt and plenty of freshly ground black pepper. Mix in the garlic, coriander and oregano. Cook the French beans until just tender. Drain and mix with the salad. Add the nuts, pineapple and prawns. Blend the fromage frais with the juice and grated zest of the oranges and gently fold into the salad.

A pretty mixture of fresh fruit makes a simple but refreshing dessert after a heavy meal. Bright and colourful, fruit salads are ideal for slimmers and can be served plain or with low-fat yoghurt rather than cream. For a really simple salad, just peel, stone, slice or chop whatever fruit you have to hand and serve in orange or apple juice. Decorate with slivers of orange rind, sprigs of fresh mint or flaked almonds or chopped pistachio nuts.

Fruit salads can be eaten at any time of the year. Pictured here are Mexican Christmas salad (far left), Winter orange salad (below left) and Green fruit salad (below). The recipes are on pages 120 and 121.

Fruit salads

Green fruit salad

175g/6oz seedless white grapes
3 kiwi fruit, skinned and diced
1 honeydew melon, balled or diced
30ml/2 tablespoons Cointreau
Syrup:
150ml/¼ pint water
75g/3oz caster sugar
rind and juice of 1 lemon

Place the grapes and kiwi fruit in a dish. Mix with the melon. Chill well. Make the syrup: place the water in a pan with the sugar. Stir over gentle heat until dissolved and add the finely pared rind. Boil rapidly for 2-3 minutes, remove the rind and add the lemon juice. Cool quickly. When cold, pour over the fruit with the liqueur. Chill for 2 hours and serve.

Italian summer fruit salad

2 peaches, stoned and sliced
4 deep purple figs, quartered
4 apricots, stoned and halved
100g/4oz hulled strawberries, preferably wild
15ml/1 tablespoon sugar
juice of 2 oranges
juice of 1 lemon
few mint leaves

Prepare all the fruit and mix in a bowl. Sprinkle with sugar and add the fruit juices. Chill in the refrigerator and serve garnished with fresh mint.

Winter orange salad

6 large oranges
150ml/¼ pint orange juice
30ml/2 tablespoons sugar
15ml/1 tablespoon orange liqueur

Peel the oranges to the quick removing all the pith. Slice thinly and place in a bowl with any juices. Use a potato peeler to peel away some of the bright orange peel and cut into thin matchstick slivers. Put in a pan with the orange juice and sugar. Heat gently over low heat, stirring until all the sugar dissolves. Pour over the oranges with the liqueur and chill well. Serve if wished with whipped cream or yoghurt.

Summer red fruit salad

175g/6oz strawberries
175g/6oz raspberries
175g/6oz redcurrants
250ml/8floz apple juice
15ml/1 tablespoon lemon juice
30ml/2 tablespoons orange liqueur
15ml/1 tablespoon clear honey (optional)
whipped cream or yoghurt
few strips orange rind

Hull the strawberries and raspberries, remove any stalks from the redcurrants and mix in a large bowl. Blend the apple juice, lemon juice and orange liqueur. Sweeten with honey if wished and pour over the fruit. Chill for at least two hours before serving. Serve decorated with whipped cream or thick yoghurt sprinkled with thin strips of orange rind.

Citrus salad with peaches

2 large oranges
2 pink grapefruit
3 peaches, stoned and sliced
60ml/4 tablespoons orange juice
30ml/2 tablespoons apricot or cherry brandy

Peel the oranges and grapefruit and cut into segments, reserving any juice. Place in a serving dish with the sliced peaches. Pour the additional juice over the top with the liqueur. Chill for 2-3 hours before serving with cream.

Mexican Christmas salad

1 apple, cored and sliced
1 banana, sliced
$\frac{1}{2}$ fresh pineapple, peeled and sliced
1 guava, peeled and sliced
3 satsumas, segmented
juice of 1 lemon
1 pomegranate, quartered
15ml/1 tablespoon brown sugar
cream or yoghurt

Toss the apple, banana, pineapple, guava and satsumas in the lemon juice. Arrange the slices of fruit on a platter. Sprinkle with the bright red seeds of the pomegranate and also with sugar. Serve with plenty of whipped cream or yoghurt.

Exotic papaya salad

2 ruby pink grapefruit, peeled and segmented
1 large papaya, peeled, seeded and sliced
225g/8oz strawberries, hulled and sliced
juice of 4 oranges
few thin slivers of orange rind

Put the grapefruit, papaya and strawberries in a glass bowl with the orange juice. Decorate with slivers of orange rind and chill well before serving.

Khoshaf

450g/1lb mixed dried peaches, apricots, prunes, pears
30ml/2 tablespoons clear honey
grated rind and juice of $\frac{1}{2}$ lemon
small piece cinnamon stick
15ml/1 tablespoon blossom water
25g/1oz pistachio nuts

Cover the dried fruit with water and soak overnight. Put the fruit and soaking water in a pan with the honey, lemon rind and juice, cinnamon stick and blossom water. Bring to the boil. Pour into an ovenproof dish and place in a preheated oven at 170°C, 325°F, gas 3 for about 1 hour. Add the pistachio nuts and remove the cinnamon stick. Cool and serve with thick Greek yoghurt.

Pear and grapefruit salad

225g/8oz canned pear quarters in natural juice, drained
225g/8oz canned grapefruit segments
in natural juice, drained
15ml/1 tablespoon gin
225g/8oz canned raspberries in natural juice, drained
15ml/1 tablespoon lemon juice
4 scoops vanilla ice-cream

Mix the pears and grapefruit segments with the gin. Chill. Liquidize the raspberries and sieve to remove any seeds. Add the lemon juice to the purée. Chill. Arrange the pears and grapefruit in 4 bowls and dribble the purée over the top. Decorate each with a scoop of ice-cream.

Exotic fruit salad

1 pineapple, peeled and cubed
1 large ripe mango, peeled, stoned and sliced
4 kiwi fruit, peeled and sliced
175g/6oz strawberries, hulled and halved
150ml/¼ pint orange juice
juice of 1 lime
slivers of lime rind to decorate

Mix the pineapple, mango and kiwi fruit in a bowl with the strawberries, orange and lime juice. Chill well. Serve with yoghurt.

Index

Acknowledgements

The Tupperware Company
This book was produced in association with The Tupperware Company, and their storage and serving containers have been illustrated throughout. If you would like to know more about Tupperware and how to obtain the products, you should contact your local Tupperware distributor. For information on how to do this, write to:
The Tupperware Company
Tupperware House
130 College Road
Harrow
Middlesex HA1 1BQ
Tel: 01 861 1819

Photographs
We would like to thank the following companies for sponsoring some of the photography in this book:
Baxters Beetroot: page 94
Cookeen: page 63
Hellmann's Mayonnaise: page 62

John West Foods Ltd: cover and pages 50, 58, 67, 86 and 122
National Dairy Council: page 114
Ocean Spray Cranberries: page 47
Pasta Information Bureau: pages 59, 70, 106 and 107
The Tupperware Company: cover and pages 2, 6, 7, 18, 19, 22, 23, 26, 27, 30, 31, 34, 35, 38, 39, 46, 54, 55, 66, 67, 78, 79, 82, 83, 98, 99, 102, 103, 111, 118, 119 and 123
Uncle Ben's Rice: pages 71, 74 and 75

Cover photograph
Special thanks are due to John West Foods Ltd for sponsoring the cover photograph and Salmagundy (also on page 67).

Illustrations
The colour illustrations of ingredients and salad vegetables on pages 10, 11, 14 and 15 and the black and white garnishes on page 29 are by Phil Evans.

Boots Cookshop
We would like to thank the Boots Cookshop for supplying some of the products illustrated on pages, 18, 19, 22, 26, 27 and 118.